Gobbet
Junior High School

Library

THE WORLD OF THE GRAY SQUIRREL

LIVING WORLD BOOKS

John K. Terres, Editor

The World of the American Elk by Joe Van Wormer
The World of the Ant by David F. Costello
The World of the Beaver by Leonard Lee Rue III
The World of the Bison by Ed Park
The World of the Black Bear by Joe Van Wormer
The World of the Bobcat by Joe Van Wormer
The World of the Bottlenosed Dolphin
        by David K. Caldwell and Melba C. Caldwell
The World of the Canada Goose by Joe Van Wormer
The World of the Coyote by Joe Van Wormer
The World of the Frog and the Toad by George Porter
The World of the Gray Squirrel
        by Frederick S. Barkalow, Jr., and Monica Shorten
The World of the Great Horned Owl
        by G. Ronald Austing and John B. Holt, Jr.
The World of the Grizzly Bear by W. J. Schoonmaker
The World of the Gull by David F. Costello
The World of the Moose by Joe Van Wormer
The World of the Opossum by James F. Keefe
The World of the Otter by Ed Park
The World of the Porcupine by David F. Costello
The World of the Prairie Dog by David F. Costello
The World of the Pronghorn by Joe Van Wormer
The World of the Raccoon by Leonard Lee Rue III
The World of the Red Fox by Leonard Lee Rue III
The World of the Red-tailed Hawk by G. Ronald Austing
The World of the Ruffed Grouse by Leonard Lee Rue III
The World of the Snake by Hal H. Harrison
The World of the Swan by Joe Van Wormer
The World of the White-tailed Deer by Leonard Lee Rue III
The World of the Wild Turkey by James C. Lewis
The World of the Wolf
     by Russell J. Rutter and Douglas H. Pimlott
The World of the Woodchuck by W. J. Schoonmaker
The World of the Wood Duck
        by F. Eugene Hester and Jack Dermid

The World of the
Gray
Squirrel

Frederick S. Barkalow, Jr., and
Monica Shorten

Illustrated with Photographs

J. B. Lippincott Company

Philadelphia and New York

U.S. Library of Congress Cataloging in Publication Data

Barkalow, Frederick Schenck, birth date
    The world of the gray squirrel.

    (Living world books)
    Bibliography: p.
    1. Gray squirrel. I. Shorten, Monica, birth date
joint author. II. Title.
QL737.R68B37   599′.3233   72–2920
ISBN–0–397–00749–3

To
Ronnie and Burton

Authors' Introduction

"Why do you study squirrels?" We've answered the question hundreds of times and in numerous ways. The simple truth is they fascinate us. Our purpose in writing this book is to present the squirrel as we see it: a lively versatile rodent, neither "good" nor "bad," a creature about which there is still plenty to learn as it strives to adapt to the bewildering changes man brings to its world.

In our respective countries we have each hunted squirrels, kept them in captivity, learned their characters as pets, weighed and measured them, stayed out in the woods from before dawn until after dusk to watch them, and collected every kind of information we could gather about them. Remembering that Shorten gained her experience of squirrels in Britain, while Barkalow is more familiar with those in the United States, the reader can usually identify which author's experiences are being described. Many observations and opinions have been shared by both authors. All photographs not otherwise credited are by Barkalow.

First-hand accounts of the gray * squirrel in the United States refer to the subspecies *Sciurus carolinensis carolinensis,* but in general the "grey" squirrels in Britain resemble *S. c. pennsylvanicus* throughout most of their range.

We are indebted to many individuals for their contributions to our knowledge of the gray squirrel. To list them all would be difficult indeed, for our study of the species spans some three decades in Britain and America. We would, however, like to recognize those

---

* Throughout the text, we have used the spelling *gray,* the preferred American usage; *grey* is the preferred British usage.—*The Editor.*

who have given recent assistance, and whom we have not been able to thank in other publications. Dr. Vagn Flyger (University of Maryland) and Harry V. Thompson (British Ministry of Agriculture, Fisheries, and Food) acted as hosts and organized extensive and illuminating tours to allow each author to visit the squirrel in the other's country, on grants from the National Science Foundation and North Carolina State University. The success of the North Carolina Umstead State Park field operation was largely due to the efforts of Professor Robert F. Soots, Jr., and we are grateful to Ray Allison, Martin J. Barrier, Carroll L. Cordes, Richard B. Hamilton, Alva H. Harris, Alan L. Kyles, and N. Britt Smith who, as graduate students on this project, made useful contributions to our knowledge. We also wish to thank the North Carolina Wildlife Resources Commission and the State Parks Division of the North Carolina Department of Conservation and Development, respectively, for funds and a research area.

We are most grateful to Dr. Isaac T. Littleton, Director, and the staff of the D. H. Hill Library, and to Mrs. Carl Smith, our typist. Marvin Williams and Duane Raver gave us assistance in preparing the illustrations, and we should like to thank them and Mrs. Frank R. Wynne, who hand-raised many of our squirrels.

Dr. Jan C. Taylor allowed us to incorporate his original observations on social structure and behavior in a British gray squirrel population. Our friend Mrs. Helene J. Waddell helped us through difficult patches by reading and listening to many squirrel stories, and John K. Terres, our editor, showed great forbearance over delays and has been a source of encouragement and inspiration.

To all these we offer our deep appreciation, and to Joan Barkalow and Alberto Vizoso, who have suffered our fanatical enthusiasm for *Sciurus carolinensis,* the "Shade-tail of Carolina."

F. S. B.

M. S. V.

Contents

THE WORLD OF THE GRAY SQUIRREL

The gray squirrel can adapt to almost any situation.

Meet the Gray Squirrel

A CURIOUS GRAY SQUIRREL investigating a transformer near St. Louis once cut the power supply to 40,000 people; some day, it is feared, a squirrel might launch a rocket by nibbling at a cable. A hungry gray squirrel broke into a Duke University dormitory, forcibly entered a vending machine, and ate a dollar's worth of nuts and crackers; yet in North Carolina the gray squirrel has been lobbied for so successfully that it is now the state mammal. The citizens of Olney, Illinois, have yielded right-of-way in their streets to the squirrel, and any unfortunate motorist who hits one gets fined $25. Pedestrian squirrels in Longview, Washington, use a special bridge, built so they can cross the road safely. Truck drivers have found them sneaking rides on interstate highways.

Man voluntarily took the gray squirrel to Australia, South Africa, and Britain where, far from being honored or prized as a game animal, it is considered to be a pest; some British timber growers have been advised not to try to raise European sycamores because gray squirrels like to peel those trees.

A gray squirrel can live up to twenty years, and by the age of three or four it is in control of almost any situation. We'd like you to meet the gray squirrel—if it hasn't beaten us to it.

Squirrels, well over a thousand kinds, live in one place or another

15

in almost all parts of the world and in both hemispheres. There are members of the squirrel family in the Arctic at 78 degrees north latitude and at the extreme tip of Africa at about 34 degrees south. Visit the desert, and there's a little squirrel on the flowering cacti; climb rocky mountain slopes, and a marmot (a kind of squirrel) may whistle at you. On the tundra and the prairie and in most forests, there are squirrels around somewhere. The very small kinds may weigh only an ounce, and the span of your hand is greater than their full length; but the hoary marmot's 30-inch-long body tips the scales at 25 pounds.

Some squirrels live in burrows, while others are believed never to come down from the treetops. Some lie dormant more than half the year, but many are active all year round, including species which feed during daylight and others which come out only at night.

Even among tree squirrels there is variety. We still do not know where these rodents first took to trees, but they were there thirty million years ago. The early ones probably developed from some chipmunklike animal that had taken to feeding in the bushes, so they are likely to have been active during the day. As quarrels over food and space became more frequent—or as they were chased by squirrel-eating birds, reptiles, or furry predators—some began to feed at night. In America, Asia, and eastern Europe today there are thirteen genera of night gliders, the "flying" squirrels; giant ones in Indo-Malaya are brightly colored and are said to glide for hundreds of yards, with their 20-inch tails streaming behind them. North American flying squirrels sleep during the day in tree holes and emerge at dusk to feed on buds, fruits, and tree seeds or on insects. They are little creatures with silky brown-gray fur and large dark eyes set in rounded heads.

Ground squirrels are active during daylight (they are diurnal) and mostly live in burrows and feed on low-growing plants, although some, like the antelope squirrel or the golden-mantled squirrel, can climb quite well. They appeared later than the real climbers, in an age when trees were scarce.

A male flying squirrel (Glaucomys volans). *The gliding membrane shows along the forearm and side.*

The most widespread of the tree squirrels is the little Eurasian red squirrel, *Sciurus vulgaris*. Millions of them live from the northern limits of tree growth south to Mediterranean latitudes, and from Ireland east to Japan. In all this wide sweep the conservative red has not evolved into other species. Its forerunners may have crossed westward from North America in the Pliocene or Pleistocene ages, when Eurasia and America were joined by a land bridge a thousand miles wide or more, which submerged only ten to eleven thousand years ago, just yesterday in the squirrel's history. Probably there was more than one period when climate and vegetation permitted squirrels to cross from one continent to another in either direction.

17

The European red squirrel, Sciurus vulgaris, *is a close relative of the eastern gray squirrel* (photo by Chris J. Smale).

In Canada and North America only one tree squirrel—the gray squirrel—emigrates. It is more similar in many ways to the Eurasian red squirrel than to the American red squirrel, *Tamiasciurus hudsonicus,* although today it is native only to the states east of the hundredth meridian, ranging from southern Ontario and New Brunswick south into Florida and eastern Texas. Within this area six subspecies have developed.

The gray squirrel was named *Sciurus carolinensis* ("Shade-tail of Carolina") by Gmelin in the 1788 edition of Linnaeus' *Systema Naturae.* Along with its larger cousin, the fox squirrel (*Sciurus niger*), it has frequently taken a part in the folk history of this country and must be familiar to all who live in the eastern states.

Everyone is ready to swap anecdotes about squirrels in the yard or park, at summer camp, on picnics and hunting trips, or at the bird feeder. There are also tales of squirrel acrobats and squirrels that outwit the hunter's stealth. But perhaps that cartoon character, Old Bushytail, is preventing us from getting to know a far more fascinating animal, one whose qualities were not designed for our amusement or approval and whose "misdeeds" are all too often desperate attempts to adapt to an artificial environment made by man.

The gray squirrel is usually described as a small game animal, reaching a total length of about 18 inches, of which 8½ inches consists of a long bushy tail. When it is fully grown, it weighs between 14 and 17 ounces, and there is no difference in size or coloring between males and females. From above, its body is a mixture of yellowish-brown and gray, with more brown showing on the head and along the middle of its back, where the coloring is darker. Its underparts are white and its ears a yellowish-white, with no pronounced ear tufts. Its bushy tail, which appears to be dark gray frosted with white, can be spread as flat as a ribbon; then it shows itself to be composed of hairs banded in yellow and black, tipped with white.

The squirrel's large dark eyes set at the sides of its head are extremely important and well-adapted aids to its arboreal life. Unlike most mammals, the squirrel is strongly diurnal and usually moves abroad only between sunrise and dusk; its retina contains only cone cells, unlike our retina, which has a mixture of cones and rods, or that of the nocturnal flying squirrel, which is nearly pure rod. These cone cells provide outstanding visual acuity, or the ability to distinguish fine detail. Each cell has a "private line" to the brain, so that vision is not coarsened by summation, as in a rod retina, where groups of cells are joined by a common or "party line" to the brain (the difference is something like that between a fine-grained photo-

The eyes of the gray squirrel (Sciurus carolinensis) *are well adapted to life in the trees.*

graph and a coarse-grained one). The reaction of a pure cone retina is much faster than that of a mixed one. If a flickering light is shone into the eye, and the frequency of flicker is increased, the retina begins by responding to each flash separately, but eventually the reactions fuse to give one prolonged response, which is called flicker fusion. Under identical conditions, the rod retina of a guinea pig has a flicker-fusion rate of 45 flashes per second, whereas a squirrel's eye will record more than 100 separate flashes a second. (Man has a slightly higher rate than the guinea pig but does not approach that of the squirrel.) Animals that move fast need eyes which are capable of rapid accommodation, and for the squirrel this must also be valuable in sensing imminent attack from aerial or ground predators.

Just as marksmen use yellow lenses in their shooting glasses to reduce glare and enhance contrast, so the squirrel has an intraocular yellow filter in the lens of its eye. All diurnal species of animals have one, usually yellow but sometimes orange or red, either in the lens, in the cornea, or in the form of colored oil droplets in the actual cone cells. It is hard to be sure what the most primitive type of filter is, but lampreys have a lens filter, a fact which suggests that this is an elementary form. Once oil-droplet filters have been lost during a period of ancestral nocturnality, they cannot be renewed; when some snakes and geckos developed from lizards (which have colored droplets) through a nocturnal phase into a diurnal phase, their filter problem was solved when they evolved yellow lenses. Thus it is still not proved whether today's gray squirrels (which have a yellow lens) were originally diurnal or whether they developed from ancestral nocturnal forms.

The lens in the eye of a young gray squirrel deepens in color as the animal gets older and serves the adult as a yellow filter. Only eyes constructed for use in bright light can afford the loss due to absorption by the filter (nocturnal squirrels have colorless lenses); the diurnal gray squirrel may benefit by seeing contrast more sharply.

The visual sensitivity of cone retinae, as in the gray squirrel, is poor, for this ability to appreciate small quantities of light, as such, is the function of rod cells, like those found in the night-adapted flying squirrel. Adaptation to the dark is about the same for gray squirrel and man, so it should not surprise us when we see a squirrel on a midsummer's night or note one feeding by moonlight in a cornfield. Robert Packard found that gray squirrels in Kansas were most active when the incident light was between 150 and 650 footcandles—the light of early morning and late afternoon on clear days, and all day long on cloudy days. Fox squirrels preferred ten times as much light. At really low levels of light, the squirrel's eyes are incapable of vision; and they have no reflecting layer (called the tapetum) to augment weak incoming light, and therefore no "eyeshine." If they had, the squirrel would not be able to see acutely by day.

The squirrel's field of vision is very large indeed; it can see all around without moving its eyes or head. This is a great advantage for an animal that is more hunted than hunting. Its eyes are set laterally in its tapering face, with the axis of each eye at an angle of 68 degrees to the body axis. This allows something more than 40 degrees of forward binocular vision. To judge distance and solidity the squirrel may also use parallax—the apparent change in position of an object when viewed from different directions. When it is about to leap, a gray squirrel raises and lowers its head rapidly while crouched for the spring; seldom does it misjudge and fail to make a good landing. If the major part of its view is seen monocularly, clues such as parallax and horizon level would be important, but a stereoscopic, or depth-perception, view is vital if the squirrel is to speed through the trees. As it enjoys visual acuity all over its binocular field, it can probably see stereoscopically all over this area, too. Under stress, its eyes protrude, which increases its field of vision.

The gray squirrel can also see above and below with little or no head movement; an adaptation that helps it to see airborne predators. Where the optic nerve enters the back of the eye there are no visual cells; this is called a blind spot. In most animals, the blind spot is on or very near the center of the eye, but the gray squirrel has a narrow horizontal stripe of a blind spot in the upper third of its eye and, since light signals are inverted by its lens system, it has an uninterrupted image of the sky.

Squirrels are said to have a power of focusing which is exceptional among rodents, and they are clearly able to see for greater distances than most. The entire retinal area can give an image as sharp as that produced by the human *fovea centralis* (the point where vision is most acute). Jan C. Taylor, a British biologist, showed that a squirrel can recognize the precise identity of another at distances of 50 feet.

The most baffling problem of the squirrel's sight concerns its ability to discriminate colors. Because it has a pure cone retina, one would expect that it should be able to distinguish many different hues; yet experimenters have had great difficulty in training squirrels in hue discrimination. They often appeared to sense brightness rather than color. At best, they could distinguish only a few colors: yellow gave them least difficulty, only sometimes could they separate blues and greens from grays, and none could tell red from dark gray. The present opinion is that it is most unlikely that squirrels have regular trichromatic vision. Their red mechanism is almost certainly different from ours.

Most people know that a squirrel can detect a handful of nuts hidden in a closed box or drawer. Its nostrils are large and mobile, and the size of its nasal cavities suggests it has a good sense of smell. When a squirrel is hunting for food which lies under several inches of snow, its nostrils can be seen dilating from several paces away. Observations of pet squirrels, marked squirrels that have been freed, and strange wild squirrels indicate that all squirrels can remember where their food cache is only for about twenty minutes—after that the store is found by odor alone. In this way, food storage benefits the local population and the species rather than any one digger.

Perhaps the gray hasn't the best nose of all its relatives. Ellwood H. McClelland, of the Carnegie Library in Pittsburgh, was able to make a comparison between the powers of a chipmunk, a red squirrel, a fox squirrel, and a gray squirrel by throwing peanuts near them,

The gray squirrel's keen nose enables it to locate food beneath several inches of snow.

and the results are interesting, although other conditions may have varied. He wrote:

The olfactory sense of the chipmunk is apparently much superior to that of any of the other squirrels observed. Neither the gray nor the fox squirrel was able to go directly to a peanut thrown ten feet away on the lawn. The red squirrel did a little better, but generally ranged around rather than proceeding in a straight line, and seemed to depend on sight. The chipmunk, at a slight visual disadvantage by reason of its size, seemed to be guided entirely by scent; almost invariably it would run or leap directly toward a peanut on the lawn, in short grass, or in a low ground cover like *Vinca minor,* and find it speedily.

As young gray squirrels eat through the first nut harvest of their lives, they learn not only to recognize nuts but to distinguish full ones from empty ones by odor alone. If there are weevils inside, a squirrel makes a close examination and appraises value by weight. H. G. Lloyd, of the British Ministry of Agriculture, wanted to discover if his pet, Squigger, used appearance, smell, or relative weight to decide if a nut was worth eating or burying or was worthless. He devised a series of ingenious tests, running one set when Squigger was seven to eight months old and another when he was thirty-four months old to see if his performance improved with age.

Lloyd began his experiment by placing one shelled hazelnut, a familiar food, in each of twenty glass tubes set on pivots so Squigger could tip them to spill their contents. He learned this in a few minutes. Then he was challenged to find a single nut placed in one of the tubes by forceps (fresh tubes had to be used because Squigger could tell which ones had previously held nuts). Since the contents of the tubes were visible, a boiled brown pebble of similar appearance was used as a check. The squirrel never once tipped this out, but after the pebble had been left among some nuts for an hour, it was quickly rolled from its tube. During the early stages of the experiment, Squigger examined and smelled all the nuts he got out. Even empty nuts received his prolonged attention and were usually opened; later he discarded them after one quick sniff. He examined nuts infested with weevils for a longer time than he did the sound ones, and when hungry he opened and ate both kinds. When he was no longer hungry he buried all of them.

When Squigger was tested again two years later, he showed that he'd become an expert. He didn't bother to touch empty nuts but went straight for good or partly weeviled ones, although they were all hidden from his view in sockets plugged with cotton. Unsound nuts and empty but plugged sockets were completely ignored. Squigger had learned to trust his nose.

Because nestlings are blind for five weeks in the darkness of the nest, they must rely on hearing, touch, and smell. When their eyes open and they come outside they learn visual recognition, but when a squirrel is not in sight, another can still follow it along the same arboreal pathway or surface trail, pausing to sniff at various points where chemical traces presumably persist. During the breeding season, animals ready to breed come together by following such trails. The males will track a female attentively, approach her carefully, and test her probable receptivity by close sniffing.

Almost nothing is known about the sense of hearing in squirrels, since their quick reactions are often due to their unusual visual powers. But the gray squirrel's ears are much longer than seems apparent. They can be furled and laid flat or extended to stand up three quarters of an inch above the hairs on its scalp. When they are at full stretch, they can be swiveled and cupped to face forward or downward, instead of sideways. In winter, the gray squirrels in the North have tufts of hair which themselves may project a further half inch, but southern forms have less, and none can rival the Eurasian red with its long ear pencils. Most of the sounds made by squirrels are community signals, intended to be audible from afar, but it would be a mistake to imagine that these cries and barks are their only

25

With ears cupped and swiveled forward, a youngster cautiously watches the photographer. Note also the length and number of the whiskers.

sounds; their low-intensity trills and squeaks and their soft, purring voices in the den are a gentle small talk.

When young, the squirrel has three pairs of milk teeth, which are shed and replaced by permanent teeth when the animal is four to five months old. Health and livelihood depend largely on the state of the teeth, and two pairs of incisors are maintained chisel sharp, as many of us have discovered to our cost. The incisors continue to grow throughout the squirrel's life and are covered at the front by very hard, orange-colored enamel, which wears slowly compared to the softer backs of the teeth, so that a sharp cutting edge persists. The lower teeth are longer than the upper ones and can be moved independently during feeding. Tooth loss or injury leads to death, as the opposing tooth or a twisted tooth will grow on unchecked, curving around to prevent feeding and perhaps eventually piercing the skull. This condition is known as malocclusion.

Some young squirrels we raised had fallen at some stage of their early life and damaged the sockets in which their young teeth were developing; two developed malocclusion and could not have fed themselves successfully. An old squirrel seen in a park with the same trouble appeared emaciated and had to lay its head sideways on the ground to get food into the back of its mouth.

26

A squirrel eating a nut sits on its haunches and presses the food between the palms and the thumb tubercles, which help rotate the nut so that it can be stripped on all sides.

In the front of each upper tooth row, the gray squirrel has a small peglike premolar. There are four pairs of rooted grinding cheek teeth in each jaw, and once food has been cut and peeled by the incisors it is passed back and ground into very fine particles here. Anyone who has examined a squirrel's stomach contents to try to identify the food eaten will know how efficient is this dental mill.

A squirrel uses its muscular tongue to eject any debris which passes the incisors. When it is feeding on peanuts it is very careful to peel off the thin brown skins; they shoot out of the sides of the squirrel's mouth like sparks from a grinding wheel.

Not too much is known about the squirrel's sense of taste. However, when offered unusual foods, captive tame squirrels often eat a little the first time and thereafter refuse to accept them, which suggests taste is employed rather than smell.

Tactile hairs sprout strongly from key positions on the body. The shiny black whiskers on the sides of a squirrel's muzzle may be as long as 3 inches, so that even the fattest squirrel should be able to tell if it is going to get wedged in a den hole. The sensitive eye is protected by signals sent along the black inch-long hairs that sprout from above and below it. The upper ones rise to the same level as the squirrel's pricked ears. Below its chin, in the V of the lower jaw, there is a bunch of white whiskers; these indicate the necessary clearance for the lower body when the animal enters a tree hollow, but they may also be useful when the squirrel lowers its head to lap in a pool of water. Just above the wrist is a particularly obvious clump of tactile hairs that point outward, for the squirrel which gets its forepaw stuck or freezes for a moment in a position from which it cannot spring away is doomed. A single long white hair rises from each of the eight nipple sites, and there are very short sensitive hairs fringing the mouth and other body openings.

Large strong feet and muscular legs carry their owner up, down, and across its leafy world. The lift-off push is provided by a hind-foot area measuring 2 by 1 inches when the long toes are spread. The area covered by the front paw is 1 by 1 inches. The feet of young squirrels, outsized in proportion to the rest of their bodies, show how necessary such equipment is for an arboreal animal. Sharp, curved claws tip each of the hind toes and the four long fingers; the thumbs have flattened nails and are themselves very short. Palms and soles are usually naked, and they sweat in hot weather or when the squirrel is frightened. The gray squirrel grows hair between the pads during the winter only in the northern part of its range.

The other diurnal tree squirrels which live in the range of the gray squirrel are the American red squirrel and the fox squirrel. The red squirrel is easily distinguished not only by its red color and smaller size but by its noisy, aggressive behavior. There are many varieties, but weights range from 5 to 11 ounces, compared to the gray's 14 to 17 ounces, and the body is proportionately smaller. Red squirrels normally live in coniferous forests, but in the Appalachians they are at home in forests of hardwoods. They are pugnacious animals and will usually bluff the larger gray. The southern fox squirrel, ordinarily about 2 pounds in weight (twice as heavy as the gray), sometimes grows even heavier; one in North Carolina weighed $3\frac{1}{2}$ pounds. This is the largest of our tree squirrels, and the species is

The American red squirrel, Tamiasciurus hudsonicus.

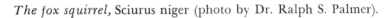

The fox squirrel, Sciurus niger (photo by Dr. Ralph S. Palmer).

variable, within and between local populations. Measurements of its total length range between 17¾ and 27½ inches. Of the three species, a pursued fox squirrel is the most likely to run for long distances along the ground before taking to the trees.

The gray squirrel appears to be the shyest. Although it becomes tame in city parks, it will rarely tolerate being stroked, unlike the fox squirrel in similar circumstances. Gray squirrels are less tolerant

29

of each other at bird feeders than are fox squirrels, but of the three the little red squirrel is by far the most aggressive; this reflects the distinctive social systems found in the three species. A threat from an enemy of another species is also met by each in a different way: a pursuing dog or cat will be thoroughly startled as a treed red squirrel comes down close to hurl defiance at it, it will be scolded by a gray squirrel at a safer distance, but it will usually get neither challenge nor scolding from a fox squirrel.

Where the three species share a neighborhood they can usually be distinguished by size alone. But in southeastern Louisiana the measurements of the gray squirrel and the smallest fox squirrel, *S. niger subauratus,* overlap, and size is not a helpful means of identification. The coloration is different; the fox squirrel has buff instead of white tips on the tail hairs. Their profiles are quite different, too: that of the fox squirrel is more acute, so that its head appears flattened, and its ears are broad and rounded. The gray squirrel has larger, tapering ears and a more rounded profile. The two can be distinguished in other ways. The small, peglike premolar tooth found in the upper jaw of the gray is absent in the fox squirrel, and the fox squirrel's long bones are reddish in color.

There are two well-known color varieties of the gray squirrel, and two less common ones. A black (melanic) form is fairly frequent in the northeastern states and in southern Ontario, Quebec, and Nova Scotia. Melanic gray squirrels were apparently more often seen than the gray form at the time of settlement of the Northeast; but Durward L. Allen, professor of wildlife management at Purdue University, has presented a vivid picture of how they gradually yielded their place to the nonmelanic color variety. Melanism seems to be partially dominant, and litters raised in Britain from cross-matings have resulted in young neither black nor gray but with dark coats having hairs tipped with brown and with tan bellies and splashes of white. Unfortunately they died before they could be mated. When hair first

Melanic phase of the north-eastern gray squirrel.

appears, these dark young could have been mistaken for normal grays, and only at about the fourth week was it obvious that they were dark. Should it be a fact that melanism is dominant, it is strange that it should be less common today, unless it is a disadvantage to squirrels when hunted by man, a black squirrel being easier to see against a tree trunk or limb. Black squirrels have been recorded in most states within the range of the northern gray squirrel, including Pennsylvania, Michigan, Indiana, Illinois, Wisconsin, Ohio, Minnesota, New York, New Jersey, Vermont, and Virginia.

A pseudoalbinistic gray squirrel uses its acute sense of smell to locate a buried acorn.

31

Gray squirrels without any pigment are known from at least thirteen states (New York, Connecticut, Massachusetts, Wisconsin, Maryland, Indiana, Illinois, West Virginia, Tennessee, Arkansas, North Carolina, South Carolina, and Alabama). It is more usual to find them in the range of the southern form. The coat is a snowy white and the eyes are ruby red in the pure albino, but more common are very pale colorings in squirrels that do not have red eyes. Albino gray squirrels have been noticed consistently in small numbers in four counties of Britain ever since the species was introduced.

No mention of white squirrels would be complete without reference to the White Squirrel Town of Olney, Illinois. The history of the population started in 1902, when a pair of "cream-colored" squirrels were trapped and brought into town. A saloonkeeper bought them and displayed them in his window, thereby attracting brisk business. A law was passed to discourage such lively advertising, and the squirrels were released. Today there is a colony of about 1200. A city ordinance gives them the right-of-way in the streets, and anyone caught killing one or smuggling one out of town may be fined $25. Every policeman and fireman in Olney has a shoulder patch on his uniform displaying the outline of the town's trademark, and an Illinois state law proclaims that it is unlawful to shoot or trap white squirrels at any time.

A cross between a pure albino and a normal gray results in young which have normal gray coloration, as Bryant Tyrell, of Takoma Park, Maryland, discovered when he had a mixed pair raising a family in his yard in 1941.

In the spring of 1946 a curiously colored squirrel attracted the attention of students on the Alabama Polytechnic Institute campus at Auburn. It was *Sciurus carolinensis,* all right, but looked as though it had been rolling in brick dust, for its coat was definitely red. It was suspected that the textile students had been trying their skills on it, but when approached it proved to be an "erythristic" squirrel in which the black pigment in the hair appears as reddish-brown or dilute cinnamon. In Wake County, North Carolina, one may expect to hear of at least one squirrel like this every two or three years. In Britain the same color phase is known, and it may well be widely distributed.

Perhaps the least common color type to occur regularly is the silver gray, in which there are few blackish areas and the brown tones are missing. Usually only one is seen at the same time and place, but anyone examining large numbers of squirrels will eventually see the type.

Sometimes hunters take squirrels which have an extra toe, finger, or leg; sometimes the number of nipples is odd, or a pair is missing.

The gray squirrel's world cannot be shown on any map which ignores its vertical labyrinths. Its varied foods must be gathered from the tops of the trees to below the surface of the earth; its shelters are built on the ground or a hundred feet up in the arms of some forest giant. It must watch for enemies down where the rattlesnake lies coiled or in the sky where the hawk sails. Once we even found a squirrel inside a largemouth bass! The squirrel is at home in the low tropical vegetation of the Florida Keys, the Spanish-moss-covered live oaks of the Gulf Coast, the oak-hickory forests of the mid-Atlantic states, the beech-maple woodlands of New England, and the river-bottom hardwoods in the prairie region. The place chosen by squirrels in all these regions will have a variety of food-bearing plants, accessible water, an abundance of natural cavities, and trees whose branches provide travel lanes from one end of the woodland to the other. Open oak-hickory forests with an understory of hazel, haw-thorn, and dogwood provide the gray squirrel with a mixture to its liking. There it can spend much of its time foraging among the litter for nuts, mushrooms, and fruits.

If the squirrel itself can't be seen, its nest almost certainly can be: a ragged ball of sticks, leaves, and twigs 1 to 2 feet in diameter,

33

This durable leaf nest was occupied continuously for more than six years.

wedged in the fork of a tree or out along a branch. Usually no entrance can be seen. Sometimes a squirrel chooses to build in a tangle of vines growing on a trunk or will fashion its home on a platform of twiggy little shoots sprouting from bole or branch. In Britain people call the leaf nests "dreys," and their silhouettes against a winter sky are the most obvious clue to a squirrel wood.

Nests are constantly repaired and added to by their owners, for

Nuts may be eaten in safety in an escape hole. Note freshly chipped bark above the entrance.

once abandoned they quickly fall to pieces. In winter natural holes in older trees are carefully investigated; if they suit the exacting standards of the wary squirrel they will become dens and perhaps shelter a group of six or seven. It is not always easy to see the entrance to a den; often a protruding scar on the trunk with a narrow darker streak on the bark below will show where it is. The entrance may be quite small—3 to 4 inches in diameter—and you can often see where squirrels have gnawed the bark around the rim of the hole. Larger ragged holes in hollow trees are more likely to lead to panic stations, not homes. A squirrel on the run will use an old woodpecker hole, rotted crevices in old snags and stumps, or even a hole in the ground. It will dive into any convenient leaf nest if there is a real emergency. Hunters often overhear a noisy debate between the squirrel owner and the uninvited guest, but if there is no protest the invading squirrel will lie low until the hunters give up.

A long life can only be earned by constant wariness, and though the squirrel has "eyes on all sides of its head" it cannot afford to spend much time hunched over its food in places where vegetation obscures its view. It prefers to eat at a table. We often find old stumps that are littered with remains of many meals: nutshells, fragments of acorns, or scales from pine cones. Failing to find a lookout post, a squirrel climbs to the first large limb of a tree with its meal and eats it there. But many foods cannot be carried to safety, either because the items are small and are gathered rapidly and devoured at a gulp or because they are part of a bulky structure such as a cluster of large pine cones.

Other animals use the squirrel's table. Some of the litter may have been left by fox squirrels, red squirrels, chipmunks, or mice. Some birds also will feed there. At dusk the little flying squirrel glides down silently, with nut in mouth, and contributes his portion to the mess. The deer mouse comes to search for fragments, leaving his tiny droppings among the shells.

The forest floor shows other signs that squirrels are around. In

35

winter the ground is honeycombed with little diggings 2 to 3 inches across and about as deep, where gray squirrels have dug up autumn stores; under pines, the needles around the lip of such holes are twisted into a circle, making it appear as if a drill had been used. Tracks found in mud or snow are usually those of a bounding squirrel, passing at speed. When running, its feet hit the ground in a cluster at intervals of about every 5 feet, but a more steady lope is shown by tracks at 10-inch intervals. At top speed the hind feet land ahead of and outside the impression left by the smaller forefeet; when going more slowly, the squirrel usually brings its hind feet down where they obliterate the tracks of the forefeet. The two pairs of feet do not strike the ground in unison, which explains why the track is not symmetrical.

A slow walk or a short hop is used while foraging. When walking, a squirrel leaves a line of single or superimposed tracks; and the slow hop leaves the easiest of all tracks to interpret, for the front feet strike ahead. Unless the mud or snow is deep and soft no heel mark is made, but claw marks are usually there. Often a squirrel spreads its toes to a span of 1 inch.

In a woodland grove early one January morning, a wet snow had blanketed the ground and coated the branches where generations of squirrels had made a highway through a line of oaks. The tree at the end of the line rose from snow patterned in every direction with trails leading to and coming from the butt. Although there were many excavations where squirrels had recently been digging out food, not one animal was in sight. Something seemed odd about the situation: there were no trails on the ground between the trees, and no snow had been knocked from the linking branches. Surely that one oak couldn't be the home of all the trailmakers around its base. But how had the others reached it? The answer was not long in coming. Soon a large female followed by two young moved rapidly through the trees, seemingly flowing along the *underside* of a branch to its snow-free tip.

36

Gray squirrel tracks on a sandbar . . .

and claw marks on a birch tree.

Each in turn then flipped upright to leap to the outer twigs of the next tree, where it continued its upside-down journey beneath the snow-blocked highway above.

Squirrel travel lanes can often be worked out by looking at the bark on trees, fallen logs, or rail fences for evidence of claw marks. Well-used routes are clearly marked, for the claws scratch, chip, or pick up the surface so that it has a different texture and often a different color. Claws find better purchase on rough bark than on the smooth young skin of beech or birch, or on a tulip poplar. Slip marks, showing three parallel scratches, crisscross over the powdery lichens on dead trees. Claw marks left by gray squirrels are usually ¼ to ½ inch apart, the length of the scratch showing how far the squirrel's

37

foot slipped before its claws engaged and held. On still, misty mornings in the woods one can often hear the rustling scratch of a squirrel's claws long before the animal can be seen.

The gray squirrel is an energetic nibbler that leaves the paired furrows of its lower incisors on the edible and inedible alike. Its lower teeth do most of the cutting, while the shorter incisors above provide a shearing edge for them to work against. The weathered shell of a box turtle, the lead sheathing on a telephone cable, the deer antler on the forest floor, and the metal identification tag on a power pole may share a common sign: the tooth marks of the gray squirrel etched deeply into their surface.

The incisors grow approximately 6 inches a year and must, as a result, be worn down. Although they can be worn against each other (their position is alternately in front of and behind the lower incisors), gnawing hard materials probably helps.

In reading signs of gray squirrels, it may be useful to try to recognize their feces. In defecating, a gray squirrel passes just a few pellets at a time, tapered cylinders with a conical projection at one end, often ⅜ inch long by ¼ inch wide. Their color is determined by the squirrels' diet. In spring, pollen from the staminate flowers of pines, oaks, and beeches colors the pellets canary yellow; in summer, wild cherries or mulberries make the pellets blackish-purple, while eating green cones produces shiny jet-black droppings; and the varied mast of fall and winter colors the pellets light or dark brown. Gray squirrels drop their pellets in a haphazard manner, so they are the least conspicuous signs of their presence.

Feces are not allowed to foul a nest, and the animal is meticulous in keeping its home dry and clean. Nestlings are frequently groomed by the mother; she licks them roughly, often causing them to defecate, and removes all their waste. The coats of baby squirrels are always spotless and glistening, and their odor is somewhat like that of a freshly opened hickory nut.

The squirrel uses its nose to gather information about other squirrels that it cannot see, as the behavior of males during the breeding season makes clear. But oddly enough, only recently has any attention been paid to another habit of the gray squirrel: scent marking. Gnawed patches of bark are familiar sights on the exposed roots of trees, among the root buttresses, under the large lower branches, and on knobs or irregularities on trunks or along the limbs. Below or beside the nibbled patch of bark is often a darker patch where squirrels have been seen to deposit a few drops of urine. Jan C. Taylor, watching the social behavior of gray squirrels in England, recognized this as a deliberate act of communication, practised by adults of either sex throughout the year but with increased frequency from late May to early June and from late August to early September. The first marking peak coincides with pairing activity, but not the second. Strange squirrels coming into an area thus scent-marked appear to be searching for marking points.

Our American red squirrel and fox squirrel appear to use similar marking points, and Taylor has seen this behavior in red squirrels in Finland. One of the easiest places to find them is the local city park, where the numerous gray squirrels post information at some point on practically every large tree.

The body odor of a passing squirrel would quickly disappear from an exposed trail, limb, or marking point were there not a mechanism for "fixing" the smell. The Cowper's gland in males has a waxy secretion which, Taylor suggests, may make the urine odor more durable. There are also sweat and oil glands on the palms and soles. Other species of animals have glands in the corner of the mouth (apocrine glands), and it is likely that squirrels also have them and use them when nibbling bark or a nut which they are about to bury. A female squirrel quite obviously has glands to advertise her breeding state. Both sexes sometimes pull themselves along the branches with their forepaws, or adopt a sitting position and shuffle along in

39

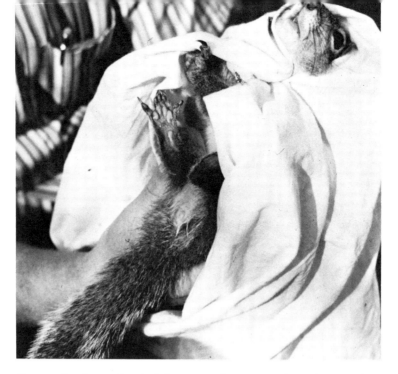

Sweat glands are located between the foot pads. When excited or hot, the gray squirrel leaves wet tracks on a dry surface.

that position, but we don't know whether or not this represents marking by secretions from anal or dermal glands.

Squirrels communicate with each other by flashing and flickering signals from the white parts of their fur; with coughs and barks, trills and screams; and by growling, chattering, and purring. They strike attitudes that are understood at once by other squirrels, and they have distinctive ways of walking that show what they are planning to do. When one squirrel stamps its feet or raises the hair on its body, another—if it is prudent—does not wait around for further developments.

Spring

THE DAYS OF SPRING are the gray squirrel's salad days. Other wild things are courting and nest building in March when spring officially begins, but most squirrels have finished their lengthy pregnancies. Woods where the wind has blustered are spiked with buds, and sappy food will soon be plentiful—the sooner the better, for buried food may be getting scarce. Mother squirrels with young to nurse may be eating for four, and they get no help; the fathers do not take care of their young.

During the first two months of spring, full-grown squirrels search desperately for food. They usually have lost weight during the winter, and now each week brings new sweet juices of plant life, rich in vitamins and growth substances. From their lowest weights in March, both males and females of the squirrel community gain steadily until May, although the gain made in autumn will be greater, if the trees fruit well. R. L. Ludwick and his coworkers at the Virginia Polytechnic Institute ran feeding trials on captive gray squirrels and discovered that a group of immatures voluntarily ate 42 percent less during the winter months of January to March than their average rations. This observation makes us curious to know if wild squirrels do the same; there are many complications which affect the behavior of caged squirrels, and out in the woods the free squirrel's natural feeding defies sophisticated assessment. It is tempting to imagine that Ludwick's squirrels, which he showed to make use of about 75

41

percent of the fuel power in their food (whether eating a lot or a little), help to tide over the hard times of winter by instinctive fasting; this would conserve the community's food supply and perhaps reduce the time each animal had to forage in the cold. The grown squirrels at VPI ate 32 percent more than was calculated as necessary to keep them going during the other seasons of the year. A similar self-imposed diet in male white-tailed deer was noticed by T. A. Long, at Pennsylvania State University, who found that they ate up to a third less of offered food from January to March, while does and young deer ate normally. It would be surprising to find that pregnant and nursing gray squirrels dieted at this time; but how convenient for them if other groups held back!

A squirrel's springtime salad of buds and the delicate flowers on maple twigs is soon garnished by early catkins from beeches and oaks. Before the pollen is dry and drifting, brisk flower-picking takes squirrels out to the tips of branches, where they lean over to cut the flowery shoots or hang head down to pull the catkins to their mouths. Under the trees, the ground is spread with cut shoots, many of which have telltale pruned flower stalks. Not many female flowers are eaten; probably the pollen of the male flower is the prize. One squirrel eating pine catkins never cut the heavy twig but just hung over its salad bowl, daintily eating one yellow spear after another.

In the woods near Raleigh, North Carolina, there was a young

Hordes of gray squirrels feast in beech trees when the male flowers are plentiful.

squirrel with a badly torn ear; even when the wound healed and she became an adult the ear stayed crumpled, making her easy to recognize. "Crumpled-ear" brought out two young her first adult spring; she had only one litter that year. The next she was chased and mated on January 17 and had her young between March 1 and 3, keeping out of sight during the interval. She was behaving very conventionally, for the winter peak in matings in the Southeast is usually in the first two weeks of January, and so far as we know a squirrel normally carries her young for forty-four days. This, followed by about six weeks of nursing, is a long protective period for a small mammal, especially since after this time a young squirrel, its eyes open only for the last week or so, still tags along with its mother and drinks milk between nibbles for the next three or four weeks. A four-month-old "tree kitten" will stay with its brothers and sisters much longer, if it can; frequently a family is still with the mother in late fall, when the young are more than nine months old.

The mothers have more young, and more families are produced, if there was a bountiful harvest of nuts and berries the preceding autumn. Then the winter broods each contain two to four young, and most of the females will be caring for nestlings in the spring. If the mast crop is poor, few families are born, and usually one to three young per litter is the best that can be managed.

A newborn gray squirrel looks rather like an hors d'oeuvre—a naked, squealing, pink hors d'oeuvre with short whiskers and little claws. It weighs 12 grams, slightly more than a fifty-cent piece. It is blind and its ears are folded down over where the ear opening will be. You can see at once why the twiggy nest is lined with bark, carefully fluffed to cradle such delicacy; the baby's skin is almost transparent.

Crumpled-ear had three young to nurse through March, April, and May, and we saw them first on April 19, jerkily creeping around the den hole. By this time young squirrels already carry parasites.

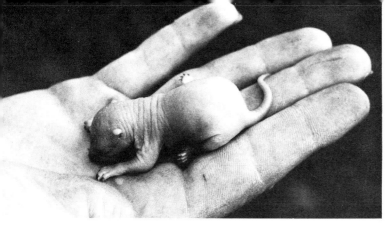

*Two-day-old gray squirrel,
tiny and pink.*

Fleas and mites and lice are likely to have explored the small, naked hosts from the time they were born, and a tiny single-celled parasite named *Hepatozoon sciuri* can be found encysted in the white blood cells of even the youngest animals. These inert blood parasites are usually found in gray squirrels of all ages and at all seasons; they appear to cause no harm.

Many squirrels, when they have young, make use of a second nest during the rearing time. It will have been inspected and prepared, or built specially, before the birth takes place, and a mother will move her young to it if the family is approached or otherwise disturbed. Sometimes there seems to be no reason for the upheaval, unless it is the enormous number of fleas in the abandoned nest.

Mother squirrels are brave in coming to the rescue when their young cry for help. Until it is about three and one half months old, the nestling has a piercing squeal which brings its mother running. Investigators handling young squirrels should keep a wary eye on the branches above. Biologists Hans Uhlig and Gordon Clark have each been bitten by a female gray squirrel turned tigress, and a female leaped down on the head of North Carolina graduate student William Miller, who had been examining her young in their nest box.

In England, we were collecting live young during one of our spring squirrel shoots designed to reduce their numbers—climbing up and taking them from nests by hand to prevent their getting bruised in falling—when our climber had a nasty moment. As he put the last nestling into his pocket it started to screech and a big female burst like a rocket from an evergreen nearby, ran down the oak branch, and sank her teeth in his hand. Chillingly aware that below he was ringed with loaded shotguns, one in the hands of his wife, he was as pleased as an astronaut to set foot on earth again! Had he left a young one in the rifled nest, there is little doubt that the mother would have moved it.

A gray squirrel moving house in an urban neighborhood appeared to be wearing a rubber collar around her neck. As she hopped down the sidewalk, the collar was seen to be a baby squirrel, held firmly in her mouth. She had grasped the hairless young by the belly and it wrapped itself around her neck. She took no notice of children playing nearby but continued her journey to the end of the walk, where she climbed an oak tree and disappeared. A closer look revealed a newly built leaf nest there. In a few minutes she reappeared, retraced her route, and climbed another tree at the other end of the walk. Seconds later she was back again with another baby held in the same manner. Altogether it took her about twelve minutes to transfer three young about 100 yards from one nest to the other.

Dr. David L. Weaver, of North Carolina State University, has described one squirrel mother he watched moving her young: Her journey took her through the branches of a mulberry tree, whereupon she wedged the baby into a crotch and proceeded to gorge herself upon the fruit. When she was full, she wiped her mouth, picked up her young, and continued her journey to the new nest. Sometimes, but not often, a nestling is left behind. During the burdened journey a mother will sometimes drop her young if her life is threatened. But she may put it down and turn to face the danger, distracting the attacker's attention.

Biologist John Nichols observed a fuzzy, half-grown gray squirrel and its mother. First the youngster became stranded on a narrow sloping ledge, twelve feet above the ground, but solved things by dropping to the ground. Soon the mother, followed by the youngster, went to a honey locust and climbed well into the branches, where the young

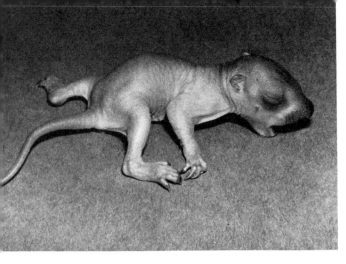

At one week, short hairs appear on head and muzzle. (The ear flaps unfolded at two days and stand away from the head.) This baby is squealing; a squirrel can squeal after only a few hours.

one stopped. The old squirrel went on farther, then came back, picked it up, and took it right up the tree out of sight.

We have never seen a mother pick up her young by the nape of the neck, although Robert J. Russell, of Lawrence, Kansas, saw a young female weighing 159 grams (about 5½ ounces) being carried like this. We *have* seen a mother seize a youngster by the leg and drag it a little until she could get a hold on the underside just behind the front legs.

A rough guide to determining the age of a young squirrel is as follows:

At one day of age, the young measure 109 to 119 millimeters * (mm) from naked nose to naked tail tip and are pink and blind with closed ears.

At one week of age, total measurement is 125 to 145 mm, and the baby has distinct whiskers.

At two weeks of age, total measurement is 146 to 162 mm, and the back of the squirrel looks dark instead of pink, with hair just beginning to show.

At three weeks of age, total measurement is 163 to 190 mm, and the squirrel has hair 1 mm long on its back. Its ears begin to open in a few days, and it has cut two incisor teeth in its lower jaw.

At four weeks of age, total measurement is 191 to 225 mm. Silvery hairs on the tail are about 2 mm long, but the underside of the tail is still bare. Its upper incisors are about to break the gum, and sometimes one or both eyes are opening just at the corners. Its body is now

* There are about 25 millimeters to an inch.—*The Editor.*

46

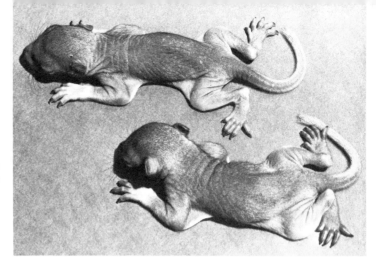

The ear canals are open at three weeks, but the eyes remain tightly closed. The body is covered with short hair.

completely covered with short hair. It is learning to stand up but is still pretty wobbly and cannot curl its tail over its back without help —although if assisted it can keep it there.

At five weeks it is 226 to 283 mm long, with hairs on the underside of the tail too; it has lower gnawing teeth 2 to 5 mm long and newly cut upper teeth, but no grinding teeth. Its eyes are open, sometimes having a misty appearance for the first day or so. A young squirrel now begins to nibble—on its nest or its family or any bark it can reach— although it is still quite dependent on its mother for milk and would not survive if abandoned.

From then onward, it is a regular squirrel in miniature. Its ears are held erect, its eyes shine, and it is capable of sitting on its haunches to free its front paws to hold food. This calls for great effort; nestlings of this age may fall over sideways and still go on nibbling. The squirrel begins to cut its grinding cheek teeth at six weeks, but it is still dependent on milk. This is rather hard on a mother with

At five weeks a gray squirrel measures 10 inches overall, about 4½ inches of which is tail. For the next month it will grow about an inch a week (photo by Jack F. Dermid).

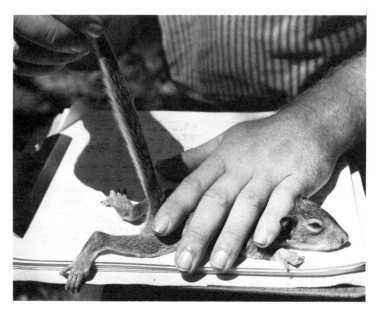

Once it opens its eyes, a young gray squirrel is very attractive. This baby has learned to stand up and is mastering the art of curling its silvery tail over its back.

three or four to feed, for their incisors are now 6 mm long in their lower jaws, and 2 mm long above, and they each measure some 284 to 315 mm from nose tip to tail tip, ignoring the hairs.

When it is about seven weeks old, the little squirrel has usually had several looks at the world outside its nest and has probably tried its new teeth on twigs and bark outside the den hole. It will have found a bud or a leaf to chew and swallow, but even now the bulk of its food is milk. Between eight to ten weeks of age, it is increasingly active outside the nest and finds its hunger satisfied more and more by solid food. Mothers with young of this age never suckle them even for a moment outside the nest, nor do the young beg to be fed outside. But when a class of students was checking our nest boxes one day, we found a box which had a mother and some open-eyed young about seven weeks old which were nursing when the box was lowered to the ground and the lid removed. Although these were wild squirrels, they continued to nurse while the students gathered around, and the mother seemed quite undismayed.

The seven-week-old young that Crumpled-ear brought out of the den that April morning were in shining health. They watched her eat a wood thrush egg from a nest that jays had robbed of all but this one, which was cracked. The egg-eating habit does not seem shared by all squirrels in one group; if it were, few birds would rear young in the woods. It seems to be an individual quirk, hit upon by accident

48

—as in this case, by finding a cracked egg—and thereafter indulged in by that particular squirrel. Very few of our caged squirrels would eat an egg; and in Britain squirrels came down a tree to feed at a trap site thirty times a day right by a wood pigeon's nest, all through the nesting season when two eggs lay in plain view on the crisscrossed twigs, and the eggs were never touched. Back-yard and park squirrels probably eat more eggs than their wild relations.

On their first outings the young try their teeth on everything and quickly improve their skill at sitting up steadily. Even Crumpled-ear's family, on what must have been their first expedition, showed some ability. When one sat back and tried to gather young leaves to its mouth in a muff-handed manner, the other two came over and joined in, butting and scrambling till the first let out a squeak of protest and a distinct chattering. A squirrel will warn others off by demonstrating its teeth (chattering) and claws (it makes rapid passes with its fore-feet, held with the fingers apart and claws displayed). Often there are angry squeaks from nest boxes when the young are jockeying for the best position.

A grown squirrel will eat about 24 ounces of nuts in a week and can cram nearly 3 ounces of food into its stomach at a time. The food is processed during its passage along no less than 7 feet of digestive tract.

Two captive squirrels in Britain were seen refecting—that is, eating their feces—a habit that is repulsive to our squeamish imaginations but plain sense to animals like the rabbit and the prairie dog which eat plant food full of cellulose. To make full use of such food, an animal must pass it through the digestive tract twice—the first time to allow bacteria in the caecum to work on the cellulose, the second time to digest the product of their work. After the first run-through a special kind of pellet, greenish and small, is eaten just as it is extruded. Refection (also called coprophagy) is a nocturnal activity, so it is rarely seen in wild animals and often missed when the behavior of captive animals is watched. One way to discover if a caged animal produces these pellets is to put a stiff flared collar around its neck to prevent refection and permit the collection of droppings, which fall through the wire floor into a tray during the night. Gray squirrels, with a caecum some 90 mm long, are well fitted for refection.

Rainfalls of spring encourage fungi to appear in the woodlands, and squirrels eat many of these. In Britain *Lactarius deliciosus*—a misnomer—often shows the squirrel's toothmarks. It is the practical joker's mushroom, since it has the curious effect of turning urine red. Body fat of British squirrels is sometimes colored a bright orange, instead of the usual cream, and this may come from eating *Lactarius* or something similar. Maple keys and elm seeds attract many squirrels to feed; the young squirrels' paws and cheeks get coated with gelatinous froth after feeding on elm, so that they get a lot of grooming practice.

John K. Terres, our editor, watched gray squirrels make full use of the red-brown flower buds on elm trees during April in Pennsylvania and New York. He was struck by the speed and eagerness of the feasting, calculating that one squirrel ate just under a hundred buds the size of garden peas in fifteen minutes.

As spring turns to summer, gray squirrels indulge in dust baths. A young squirrel will hop to a patch of dry sand, push its nose into it, then turn its head as a cat does when rubbing against you. Within half a minute, the squirrel has rolled about in the sand, kicked out its legs, pulled itself around in circles, and given one convulsive leap before flicking its tail and running off. Views differ on the reasons for such wallowing. Jan C. Taylor saw it twenty-three times during his study of gray squirrel behavior in Britain and found that it happened most often in June. Both young and old males and females would dust bathe, but adult females were most addicted. Taylor thought it probably had something to do with marking activities, for he noticed that it usually happened near a squirrel marking point. But Doris Hauser, of Fayetteville, North Carolina, saw a different significance when she happened to notice a gray squirrel which had apparently gone mad in her back yard. It was a sunny, warm day in July when nests of large harvester ants were boiling over with activity, with many winged ants coming out and yellow-shafted flickers going from one ant mound to another. The squirrel appeared near the center of this scene, only twenty feet from Mrs. Hauser's window. It dug up soil with its forefeet, pushed its muzzle into the ground, then settled down a-sprawl. Suddenly it rolled, turning somersaults and leaping wildly before sprawling again. On successive days a single squirrel arrived and claimed the sand patch, threatening any others which approached and chasing them away if they got too close. Mrs. Hauser examined the ground where the squirrel had been and each time found ants in the soil.

"Anting," believed to be an attempt to fumigate feather lice with the acid sprayed by ants, is common among birds, but very few people agree that other animals indulge in the act. Yet Mrs. Hauser is a careful observer, and her account is most convincing.

Growth, a biological handbook, puts the gray squirrel into the same longevity class as the reindeer, the timber wolf, the coyote, and the chicken for living to a ripe old age of fourteen to fifteen years. Two albino gray squirrels kept in captivity for twenty years by W. C. Koon of Monongah, West Virginia, probably still hold the record for greatest known age. There are many accounts of captives surviving for more than twelve years, and some up to eighteen years, when they are sheltered from natural enemies and disease and housed and fed adequately.

There is a vast difference, however, between surviving in captivity and in the wild. A captive squirrel's old age may depend on the state of its cheek teeth; as long as they are fit to grind, it will probably thrive, though its vision may be impaired by cataracts and its once graceful

To the gray squirrel, happiness is a permanent brook, an open forest floor, and gnarled oaks, beeches, hickories, and maples.

movements slowed to a shuffling hop. The wild squirrel, subjected on every hand to enemies, diseases, accidents, an inconsistent food supply, and rigorous climatic conditions, is unlikely to reach an age at which tooth wear becomes important to its survival.

The life expectancy of wild gray squirrels was one of the many things we studied on our research plots in Umstead State Park, near Raleigh, North Carolina. This area is typical of the northern Piedmont region, with ridges clothed in oak, hickory, red maple, and pine, and ravines of beech and maple. Under this canopy there are dogwoods and sourwoods, and squirrels find den sites in massive oaks and towering tulip poplars. Protected from logging and hunting for more than three decades, the 5,200-acre park has the appearance of continuous pristine woodland. The gobble of the wild turkey at first light and the ghostlike movement of a white-tailed doe and fawn from the bedding thicket at dusk mark the beginning and the end of the squirrel's day. The only human interference with its world has been the addition of nest boxes on one half of the research area during part of our twelve-year study.

We followed the fate of 1,023 known-age squirrels marked between 1956 and 1965. When Richard B. Hamilton, one of the graduate students, worked out the life table, he found that only 25 percent of the young squirrels born were likely to be found there a year later, contradicting earlier claims that many young survived because of

52

the long months of sheltered development. Some of the missing 75 percent moved to other areas miles away, to settle down and raise their own families (it may be that such dispersal is more often a habit of young animals than of adults), but in this extensive forest, squirrels maintain a fairly stable population. Hamilton believed the annual dispersal rate for all age classes is about 15 percent.

Although many of the young are lost, the ones that live to become adults have twice as good a chance of surviving. If they successfully reach their second birthday, they have an excellent chance of living to celebrate their fourth, and only when they are seven years old do their chances of living an additional six months or more become slim. A female squirrel has a slightly better prospect of reaching old age than does her mate.

If there were such an animal as the "average" gray squirrel, it could expect to live for one year after it is born. But when we met and marked Miss D5, as a hairless seven-day-old nestling, she was no average squirrel. Much later, we greeted and released her for the fifteenth time at the venerable old age of eight years, ten months, and twenty days, and she still appeared to be in the prime of life. It would be neat if on our longevity charts the prizewinner were a female, but twenty days later she was outdone by C2; he showed up just five days before his ninth birthday. As far as we know, these two squirrels hold the record for survival in the wild.

It is easy to say that squirrels die, but it is another matter to list all the various causes of their deaths and to judge how important one cause may be in the sum of deaths throughout the community.

Rattlesnakes appear to relish young squirrels. A timber rattler killed near Bellamy, Alabama, was found to have one in its stomach, and a 5-foot diamondback rattler killed near Thomasville, Alabama, when cut open, contained two fully grown gray squirrels. William Byrd remarked upon a similar find in North Carolina in 1728: "By the way, one of our men kill'd another Rattle-Snake, with 11 Rattles, having a large Gray Squirrel in its Maw, the head of which was already digested, while the Body remain'd Stil entire."

On our North Carolina research area we have no rattlers, and only our copperheads, black racers, rat snakes, and king snakes are large enough to be a possible danger to squirrels. We occasionally found black rat snakes in the nest boxes, and once we removed a big one, over 5½ feet long, that had just swallowed two six-week-old squirrels whole, suffocating them in the process. Red-tailed hawks take a number of squirrels of all ages; one watched us release a tagged squirrel and then swooped and picked it out of the treetop as it was making off. We found a seven-week-old animal in the nest of a barred owl, and a freshly killed six-year-old was discovered partly eaten by a predatory bird—possibly the great horned owl that lived nearby.

Our research work in the area may have helped other predators to capture squirrels. We knew a red fox took one squirrel from a trap, because we found its characteristic fox hairs with the squirrel blood and hair.

Some young squirrels are attacked by their own kind, and when we find partly eaten young in the boxes we suspect that gray squirrels themselves are often responsible. Students brought in a two-week-old nestling which bore neat tooth marks; their professor happened to be in the painful position of being able to compare these with fresh marks on his own fingers.

During the spring, winter dens and nest boxes that have been vacated may be put to use by other species. Little screech owls, yellow-shafted flickers, and tufted titmice all reared families in our squirrel boxes. Bees took over for the summer and built their honeycombs, but squirrels reclaimed possession when the bees died off in the winter. In England, gray squirrels reared young in boxes which had been put up for tawny owls; and great tits, starlings, and jackdaws built in empty squirrel boxes.

Even the squirrel's leaf nest attracts visitors. A raccoon may find

A litter nest of beech leaves and twigs. The shredded-bark inner lining hanging on the twigs at the lower left is evidence that a raccoon has investigated it.

one and eat the squirrel's brood, tearing out the nest lining as it does so. In late spring, a raccoon will sometimes be seen stretched out on the top of a squirrel's nest to bask in the sun. Furred animals lying in the sun are doing more than passing the time pleasantly and uselessly; vitamin D forms on their hairs which is then either ingested during grooming or absorbed directly; humans form it on the surface of their skin. The squirrel's liver can store enough D for several months, and in fact a surplus is usually formed so that 70 percent may be excreted with the feces. Vitamin D is vital for healthy animals because of its well-known function in calcium absorption and formation of calcium phosphate in the blood, and it is especially important for pregnant and lactating squirrels and for bone development of the young.

In early May we can expect to see one or two young squirrels a day lying flattened on the mile-long road to the campus, and a few adults get killed by traffic each week. Even though the rather artificial habitat and behavior of this population may exaggerate the total kill on roads, the national figure must be very high during the two seasons when young begin to roam.

55

Summer

Now THE WOODS are leafy mazes of sunlight and shadow. The trans-formation has been going on gradually throughout the spring, but go away for a while and on returning you will find a new world. Eyes peer from hidden watchtowers to glimpse a movement; ears listen to the sounds of life on every side and sift alarms from the rustle and buzz, the scratching and pattering, the calling of busy creatures. The air is full of scents as well as sounds, signposts in the language of each species.

Crumpled-ear lies spread-eagled on the warm bark of a branch, eyes half closed, tail limp, paws soft and relaxed. Ears and nose move slightly now and then, for even this sleepy, sun-soaked animal is ready to leap for her life if danger signals. The silver-gray coat of winter was molted out by early June, after her young were weaned, and her coloration now blends so well with that of the olive-brown bark that unless a summer breeze moves her feathery tail you might never see her.

As the woods become more leafy and dense, the squirrels become slimmer and sleeker. The mother squirrel is now a yellowish-brown, with bright reddish splashes along her flanks and on the backs of her hands and feet. Palms and soles have lost every trace of woolly hair, and they perspire slightly. Her ears appear naked, although close examination reveals a sparse covering of short brown hairs, but the white cushion of soft hairs behind her ears has gone, together with the modest ginger ear tufts. She is better fitted for summer, but with the outlines of her head and body more closely revealed she has lost some of her charm. She is more of a rodent and less of an "arboreal kitten." Her tail, so generously plumed in winter, has lost some silver and white, and toward the end of July it will be very thin and ragged as the old hairs fall.

Replacing the old coat has taken about six weeks, and this process occurs twice a year. During the spring molt, changes begin on the head and shoulders and move backwards; in the fall the direction is reversed. The hairs of the tail are changed only once a year, surviving from August to August. The new short growth may first appear among the old hairs at the tip of the tail, but there are many exceptions.

The youngsters born in the winter had nestling coats like the mother's winter coat; they molted as soon as they were weaned and made their appearance in complete summer pelage in May. Before this, they seemed to be wearing woolly pants, for the rough, dull baby fur on their hips and hind legs stood out in contrast to their sleek foreparts. Not all of the scratching that went on at this time was due to the presence of parasites; a lot of the loosening hair was vigorously scratched out, and nests contain drifts of shed hair at molting time.

The family still shares the winter den, but life there cannot be too comfortable. The three babies are more than half grown, and the squeaking and yelping suggest that it is no longer easy to please everyone as they settle down for the night. During her pregnancy the fleas the mother carried also bred, so that each youngster took over a troop of them. Lice and mites add to the discomfort, and the mother squirrel becomes increasingly restless as hormones prepare her for another season of breeding.

Many of the leaf nests that are used in summer were repaired and lined with shredded leaves or bark in the winter by pregnant squirrels, as alternative refuges for the family. But from late May into July there is another burst of building activity, by the winter-born

To line a summer litter nest, the pregnant female shreds inner bark with her incisors until it becomes a soft springy cushion to receive her young.

young, whose first attempts result in more twigs and leaves on the ground than incorporated into the nest, and by females about to have their summer litters.

One day Crumpled-ear was seen examining an old leaf nest perched on a sprouting limb stump. She pruned a few shoots and pushed them one by one inside the nest. In the afternoon she took hickory leaves, bunched in her mouth, on four journeys up the tree and went into the leaf nest with them. She had been stripping bark from a tulip poplar branch only a few days before; at the time we assumed that she was simply adding to the lining of her winter nursery nest, but her behavior now meant that either she was pregnant or she was about to go into oestrus. Although, during the late spring, females with young often move them to a different leaf nest, these alternate homes are not usually lined with bark.

Not all females bear two successive litters of young in a year, for many different factors interact to regulate the breeding condition of individuals in a community of squirrels. Crumpled-ear was now in her second year of breeding. With an abundant harvest of acorns and hickories, she had passed the mild winter in excellent condition and found little hardship in suckling her brood of three. Since the young were born early in March, she could have left them earlier; they would have had a fair chance of survival. But until these first summer days they had shared the old den, and during their early expeditions the mother accompanied them, keeping them close to the den tree. Now they fed and played together without her constant presence.

58

A young family's first pioneer journeys are sometimes undertaken while the mother is away feeding. Such explorations, although crowded with new experiences, take the youngsters only to the den mouth or a few inches outside. First there is the light to get used to, the strange far-off sounds, and the mixture of new scents. Blinking and trembling, noses quivering, they meet the world outside. They peep and duck back again the first few times, but squirrels are full of curiosity. One day when the mother returns she will find her young scrambling up to meet her as she squeezes into the den mouth, and after they nurse they will still move restlessly around until she leaves the den and waits for them to follow.

At first, young females are more venturesome than their brothers. They are often heavier throughout the pre-weaning period, more successful at feeding time, and better at seeking out the most comfortable position in the heap of young. In a mixed litter the males seem to hang back during family outings and to return to the den area more often. All the young squirrels return to the mother, to sniff and touch her, after they have been away from her side for a while. It might seem that they were begging for milk (for they are only partly weaned) or begging to be picked up and carried, but a more likely reason is that they are learning to recognize her visually. A soft sputtering purr is exchanged when they meet. The mother also has a summoning call, sounding like a short cough, which brings her family away from exposed wanderings to the safety of cover.

When a young squirrel finds something new and attractive, it will give the most eloquent display of curiosity battling with caution. One hind leg stretched backward, claws dug in for instant retreat, the baby edges jerkily toward the mystery. Its little tail is laid forward along one side of its body. It leaps backward once or twice, craning forward again to sniff, its tail trembling or flicking nervously. If the object remains quiet, the baby becomes bolder; should its extended nose tell it that this thing is richly edible, then what a change in be-

A youngster finds its first pecan hard to crack.

havior! Grasping it between its teeth, the baby lifts it, transfers it quickly to its hands, rocks back on its haunches, and then, after rotating the food quickly between its short thumbs, starts to nibble. When it has finished eating (with much spitting aside of inedible remains), it drops the leftovers and makes a quick search for more. Then the delightful bumbling, purring sound of the happy baby can be heard. It is probably the same sound that coaxes the mother to allow suckling.

Much of the play of young squirrels involves racing at maximum speed up and down and around the tree trunks and along the branches, wrestling with litter mates, and leaping in all directions. Tactics are perfected for fending off would-be attackers. Serious fights between adult gray squirrels are more unusual than one might suppose, and disputes are commonly settled by rituals of lunging, chasing, and scolding. If cornered and provoked, even very small nestlings will lunge, striking out with their forefeet and opening their toothless mouths widely. The same behavior persists into adult life, accompanied by squealing and the chattering of teeth, but the aim seems to be to surprise and dismay and it usually succeeds in driving away the offenders.

Besides the leaps that carry a gray squirrel from branch to branch (a full-grown animal can launch itself across a 6-foot level gap between two trees), youngsters in play practice a different leap. It looks so like an expression of sheer high spirits, "jumping for joy," that its serious purpose might be overlooked. When wrestling, the young often spring apart, leaping upward and backward or straight up and down in the same place. There is none of the preliminary sighting or the bunching up with rapid foot movements that goes on before a difficult jump. A solitary young squirrel may be seen leaping in this way when all alone on a lawn, or it may come down a tree, touch the ground, and leap backward with a half twist to catch the trunk. In the air, the body is arched so that head and feet point straight down, and the ears are laid flat. This maneuver is excellent for escaping enemies on the ground.

The basic behavior patterns of the gray squirrel are instinctive, and most of them develop in captivity, even when the baby squirrel has seen no other squirrel. What is important when the family comes out of the den is practice: practice in the quick, sure interpretation of any situation, practice in agility and speed in carrying out the correct response. Learning is largely restricted to becoming familiar with the home range and mastering the rules of social behavior as they apply there. This last is important: many hand-reared squirrels die when released in the woods because they find themselves strangers, unable to deal with the social pressures of the wild residents.

There are so many things for the young gray squirrels to practice. They must find and sample a wide range of foods, learn about water, and discover how to open hard nutshells, a skill that is very difficult for a twelve-week-old squirrel to acquire. (Many days pass before they master the nick-and-split method of neatly halving a hazelnut.) The young must also practice burying nuts and finding those already buried; they must become skillful at gathering nesting material and carrying it in their mouths while swarming up a tree; they must know

An eight-week-old squirrel on an exploring expedition.

the alarm calls of species other than their own, and the sources of greatest danger. They must become adept at racing to unexposed positions from wherever they may be and then learn to keep themselves hidden. They must remain motionless, although keyed up for flight, while a predatory animal scans with eyes, nose, and ears to discover them.

In play, young gray squirrels practice moving crablike around a tree, flattened against the bark. This skill is useful later when they may be treed by a fox, a coyote, a dog, or a man, or attacked by a hawk or an owl. Although the enemy circles the tree, looking for them, they keep hidden by shifting softly round the sheltering trunk.

To be caught on the open ground is very dangerous for squirrels. The mother will not allow her family to go to the ground until they have spent about a week in the aerial safety of the den tree. Should they attempt to descend on their own, she will hustle them back, giving her peremptory cough. When they do go down, they go as a family group. They soon learn to carry food gathered on the ground to raised lookout points—a stump or a stone wall—if it is going to take some time to eat. They obviously learn, before starting to eat, to size up the possible escape routes. Only the very young get flustered and cast about wildly looking for a ladder when startled!

This litter of eight-week-olds stays close to the base of the den tree.

In 1960, biologist J. P. Hailman provided an eyewitness account to illustrate the supervision of young by the female:

An adult, followed by three young, descended a tree head-first. Each time the female stopped, the young squirrels moved in and sniffed her back and sides, pushing each other aside. This behavior continued when they reached the ground. No "play," as such, was observed in the animals, although they often scrambled over one another on the ground in order to keep close to the female. The adult hopped to a nearby fence, which she climbed easily. The first young squirrel to follow was clumsy, but successful, and immediately went to the female and sniffed her sides. The second young animal to attempt the ascent fell twice from the half-way point, and gave up. The third individual, continually watching the adult, did not try to climb the fence. About a minute later, the adult and the first young animal rejoined the other two on the ground; the group began foraging across the grass together, with the three young squirrels intermittently sniffing the female.

Several things are clear in this description: the example set by the mother being on the borderline of possibility for the brood, the olfactory confirmation of visual recognition, the closeness of the group, and the practice in escaping from the ground.

The young squirrels must learn to follow and place scent trails and also to interpret those markings which mean "Keep out!" They will

63

A gray squirrel examines a scent mark.

have to learn to respect the rights of powerful resident squirrels, especially pregnant and nursing mothers, through whose territory they may wander.

Those slow to learn all this—the incautious ones—will vanish before winter comes.

When it is small, blind, and without experience, the baby is unavoidably left defenseless when the mother has to leave the nest to seek food for herself. If the den has too large an entrance or is too low or has been carelessly chosen in some other respect, the young may be taken by a natural enemy. Again, if they are in a leaf nest which has been poorly constructed or badly placed, they may be killed by some predatory animal. Females have been known to return and attempt to defend a nest while it was being examined by a human; they have been known to move their young to another place after some enemy has investigated the nest or when the nest has been loosened from its moorings by storm, gunshot, or shaking. But the generalized defense against peril is again instinct and practice in choosing safe positions and in building securely.

When squirrels are young, both sexes spend time practicing nest building. In July, many of the trees in a wood contain saucer-shaped platforms of freshly cut leafy twigs that have been clipped from tree branches by young gray squirrels. Some of these first "nests" fall to pieces quickly; others may last the long summer through. They may be placed high or low, out in the thinnest branches or in more stable positions. One squirrel may build a series of nests; those we have examined contained a mere handful of green leaves as a lining. Hans Uhlig noted peaks of leaf-nest building in West Virginia in July and again in mid-fall and concluded that this represented the concerted nest-building efforts of the eighteen-week-old young from winter and summer litters respectively. This theory was reinforced by the relative agreement between the numbers of leaf nests built and the proportion of young in the samples taken by hunters the following season.

Far from being a lifeless mass of dead leaves and twigs, a squirrel's nest is an active ecosystem—a world of its own. One graduate student, Alan L. Kyles, collected 104 species of arthropods from the squirrel nest boxes on our research area: 65 species of insects, 32 species of mites and ticks, 4 species of spiders, 2 centipedes, and 1 pseudoscorpion. Only 6 of the species collected were known parasites of the gray squirrel. Larvae of the gray squirrel's special flea, *Orchopeas howardi,* are particularly abundant in the nest lining. A friend once asked for the debris from a nest box to see if his flea-hatching apparatus was in good working order. No eggs or larvae were apparent in the handful of litter he was given, but it produced over 300 fleas. Mammals play host to about a thousand different kinds of fleas, and those from squirrels (and perhaps some rats) probably gave rise to the 55 kinds of fleas that live on birds. Squirrels' fleas are found in birds' nests even in areas that have been deserted by squirrels, and bird fleas have been found in squirrels' nests.

The fleas are eaten by various kinds of beetles, which therefore come to the nest, too. Histerid and Staphylinid beetles have often been found in gray squirrels' nests in Britain. The mat of debris making up the floor of an established nest attracts growth of fungi and bacteria and small insects, and there are mites, which are more attached to the squirrel's bedding than to the animal itself.

Ticks are a scourge of the squirrel in summer. In suburban areas the common dog tick, *Dermacentor variabilis,* is often found on them. In woods and forests, deer ticks are frequently able to transfer to the gray squirrel.

When a squirrel finds man's litter strewn around a picnic site, it often incorporates some into the building of its nest. We have found pieces of cloth, cord, Kleenex tissues, and even kapok in nest linings. In Britain, our pet black squirrel used a lot of energy (while we were sleeping off our Christmas feasting) in taking down the Christmas decorations and transferring them to her nest. She also did her best to remove our hair for the lining!

The squirrels use their leaf platforms during the day for resting between bouts of feeding and exploration. They also use them as refuges to crouch in until danger threatening from below has passed. It is doubtful whether they can be safely used for sleeping at night; a hole in a limb or the trunk of a tree affords better protection from owls and raccoons.

Leaf nests of another kind are built by older squirrels. They are more durable and afford all-round cover. Usually they are placed close to the main trunk of the tree, either in vines or where the trunk divides or the old stump of a branch has left a platform. Sometimes they are built in the forks of sturdy branches. Construction begins with a platform of leafy twigs, but more and more material is piled upon it until a rough mass of twigs up to a foot or more in length has reached an external diameter of perhaps 12 to 18 inches. The builder —or builders, for two squirrels have been seen collaborating—will dive and wriggle into the middle of the heap, using hands and mouth to tug and bite, and, judging by what can be seen from a distance, the cavity is shaped by repeated body turns. Leaves, bark, and sometimes moss or grass are carried into the cavity; when shredded, these materials provide a soft, dry lining.

The internal cavity of the leaf nest is somewhat elastic, but a rough average measurement would be a diameter of 4 to 5 inches for the cavity. The domed roof is windproof and waterproof, as are the walls, and the floor gradually becomes a thick mass of close-pressed debris. Whole skeletons of squirrels have been found embedded under an inch or so of flooring. Once the squirrel is inside, it can close the rough opening by a few quick movements of the forepaws and muzzle, rather in the way it pulls and pushes ground litter over a buried nut. (An old female was seen to do this from outside when she left her newborn young and went off to feed.) When the nest is built close to a tree trunk, the opening, when it is apparent, is usually toward the top of the nest on the side nearest the trunk. Litters of young were found many times in leaf nests during August on our research areas.

If a gray squirrel nest in a den hole is smelly and littered with droppings and nuts, it has probably been abandoned and then taken over by a flying squirrel. Flying squirrels may be beautiful little creatures, but they rate low on hygiene in the home.

Gray squirrels can be called omnivorous, as their diet includes animal, vegetable, and mineral materials. Those which have taken out British nationality feed heavily on caterpillars in the leaves of the oak woods in early summer. In a "caterpillar year" in England, as in the United States, one walks through the woods to an accompaniment of constant pattering, as millions of tiny droppings fall from the canopy overhead. *Tortrix viridana,* the green oak moth, is the best-known British culprit. The larvae (caterpillars) of the winter moth, *Operophtera brumata,* assist in occasionally defoliating a tree so that a second crop of leaves must be produced in July; gray squirrels find pupae of *O. brumata* in the ground and eat these too. The caterpillars destroy flowers as well as leaves and can cause a failure in the acorn crop. In Britain alone there are about a hundred oak-eating species of caterpillars.

In the United States, W. J. Hamilton of Cornell University saw

"Tree rat" habitat in Great Britain. Oak-moth caterpillars add variety to the diet of this unwelcome import from America.

squirrels feeding on gray geometrid caterpillars they pried from bark crevices in a white oak. Another year, he saw a gray squirrel eat about a dozen *Phigalia titea* caterpillars from low branches of a hickory.*

One morning in mid-June Crumpled-ear was feeding on wild strawberry fruits in a clearing. Few squirrels can resist strawberries, and another approached the same patch within ten minutes—but with the typically wary, tiptoe walk of an interested male. Crumpled-ear was obviously in pre-oestrus or oestrus condition. The male had enlarged scrotal sacs, the dark, almost hairless appearance of which showed up clearly against the rest of his white underfur. His tail was flicking in quick little waves as he hopped slowly to her, then tried to stretch his nose beneath her tail.

It had been months since Crumpled-ear had allowed any squirrel other than her young to come close; she had bitten one yearling at the base of its tail when it strayed into her den tree. But now she just turned her shoulder to the male and finished her strawberry. Then she loped off and sat on a low branch to lick her forepaws and groom her face.

The male went over the ground where she had been, making a meticulous inspection of leaves and twigs she may have sat on. Then

* The caterpillars of a moth, the so-called half-winged geometer *Phigalia titea*, are flesh-colored, about 1½ inches long, and feed on the leaves of oaks and other deciduous trees. They are active in the eastern United States from May to July.—*The Editor.*

he looked around, hopped deliberately to the tree which sheltered her, and climbed a few feet up the trunk, holding his head at a sharp angle to watch her. He flicked his tail and gave the *chuff-chuff* which many people call "a buzzing sound" (this noise almost always means that the female is in, or very near to, breeding condition).

Crumpled-ear went up about twenty feet and sat backed up against the trunk, her tail over her back and her paws folded in against her chest. The male did not follow her but watched intently. The female fidgeted with her forepaws and then gave two preliminary flicks of her tail and started calling, a rapid chucking followed by a harsh mew. Both animals then froze in a trance for several moments. The time of the mating chase had come. The male balanced along the horizontal branch and pulled himself several yards up the trunk toward her. He was chuffing. Another bigger squirrel arrived on an upper branch in a tumult of leaves, and at that the female took off, with the two males following.

They were out of sight several times, but the sound of claws tearing into bark as they doubled and circled around was clear, and the tips of the branches were shaking. Then there was a harsh scream and all other sounds ceased. The two males were crouched on different branches of a tree that held a leaf nest, with the bigger male only a few feet from the opening into which Crumpled-ear had gone. Unless a more dominant squirrel appeared on the scene quickly, he seemed likely to become the new father.

A dominant male will exert his authority over other suitors, and only in his temporary absence (through falling or being outwitted by the weaving and doubling of the female) will other males get to lead in the chase. Some of the less dominant squirrels give up and go off to look for other prospects, and gradually the affair becomes a courtship rather than a harum-scarum free-for-all. Only then is it usual for mating to take place.

Next day Crumpled-ear found herself cornered. The male that

had been in the lead of that first chase had by now discouraged the others. He faced her—his tail waving slowly, backward and forward over his ears, then circling from side to side. He touched her with muzzle and forepaws. She chattered her teeth and began to turn away but the male grasped her firmly. A man with a knapsack on his back came up the path below the tree at that moment; he did not notice the squirrels, nor they him, but when his dog came along a minute later it knew the squirrels were there and set up a tremendous barking. In a sudden scramble, the squirrels almost fell, and there was a wild rasping of claws as they raced for the upper branches and froze, each flattened on a different branch.

So Crumpled-ear started a second family fourteen weeks after the last had been born. She went back a few times to the old den tree, but only two of the young were there. One had been killed by a fox in broad daylight. So incautious had it become, gorging on berries along a leafy bank, that it had neither heard the vixen approach nor used the lightning speed needed to leap from danger and escape.

One morning Crumpled-ear was feeding in a maple which still had juicy winged seeds. Two other squirrels were feeding there, littering the ground below with empty wings. One, a yearling male, approached her and gave the rasping buzz of interest that foreshadows a chase. She turned on him, snarling and chattering her teeth so viciously that he slipped and lost his footing. His tail fluffed out like a bottle brush, and he clung in a fork, biting and tearing at the smooth bark until he laid bare small patches of the white wood. Crumpled-ear was no longer receptive.

She now defended her nest as she had previously defended her den. If any squirrel seeking refuge tried to dive in, she gave a warning storm of cries. Toward the end of July she bore a litter of four young there. Why she had changed her home is hard to tell: she could have driven her two winter young away from the den tree, as other females have done when they become pregnant again. Perhaps the young, gnawing on the wood at the den entrance, had so enlarged it that it no longer seemed safe. Perhaps a period of using the leafy platforms for resting and basking had made her less satisfied with the itchy discomfort of a den shared with the ectoparasites of a whole family. Some advantages that the den had held in winter were now of less importance: a canopy of leaves above the nest shielded it from the eyes of sailing hawks, and it was not so exposed to the unbroken force of any wind that might blow. In Britain, where introduced gray squirrels have fewer predators than in their home country, more young are born in leaf nests than in dens, even in winter.

Just as in winter, when 75 percent of the young are born within two weeks of each other, so in summer there is a peak in the birth of young gray squirrels during the last ten days of July and the first few days of August. Summer litters are significantly larger than winter litters. Over a ten-year period on our North Carolina research area 295 summer litters averaged 3.06 whereas 152 winter litters averaged 2.47 young per litter. Luckily for the species, the timetable of breeding is not inflexible. It varies a little from place to place in the same season, and it quite definitely varies from year to year if food and weather conditions have departed from average. If winter breeding has been very poor, a mild spring followed by a summer with good yields of seeds may be notable for almost continuous breeding—until a very large proportion of the females have had a litter. Summer-born young are delivered before the end of July in average years, and nursing is over by the second week in October. Full attention can then be devoted to the mast harvest, for the majority of female squirrels are in anoestrus during the fall, and the males, too, experience a regression in sexual activity. There is no 100 percent conformity with this timetable. Late pregnancies do occur, a few females have been known to bear three litters in a twelve-month period (although we doubt that all have been raised), and some males with fully developed testes have been found in every month of the year. Thus physiological and behavioral norms at the season of harvest lead to maximum use of the mast crops, while the manner of congregating to bury surplus supplies and the ability of any squirrel to locate and use the stores is of obvious value to the species.

Even during the pleasant days of summer, the gray squirrel cannot relax its vigilance. Adults and young may be killed by a variety of animals, but it is difficult to come to a conclusion about the order of importance of these predators. Snakes, foxes, skunks, stray cats and dogs, red-tailed hawks, broad-winged hawks, marsh hawks, goshawks, and Cooper's hawks all catch squirrels, especially when they are on open ground. Weasels and fishers take them, and since they also climb they may rob both nests and dens. Mink have been known to take adult squirrels, and barred owls, which use hollow trees, undoubtedly come upon litters. On our research area, the raccoon was perhaps the most serious predator of young in the nest.

Man not only causes the death of squirrels directly when he is hunting them or driving his car along the highway, he kills some indirectly by allowing his dogs and cats to run in the woods and by leaving his pool half full or his water cistern uncovered. But all this is as nothing compared with the effect man has had in altering for his own ends the common environment.

Autumn

THE GOLDEN DAYS of fall rise from misty beginnings, spreading colors at the wood's edge to burn in the clear light of noon, and squirrels are everywhere gathering their harvest. More squirrels may be seen now during an hour's walk than at any other time of year, many of them feeding in groups. So strong is the drive to eat and to store the surplus that feeding spells are prolonged and some points of normal social etiquette are relaxed.

The summer-born gray squirrels emerge into a very different world from that which awaited their predecessors in springtime. The population is at the annual high, not yet depleted by hunting and winter, and feeding brings them into more contact with other squirrels. Killing frosts and gusty winds will soon strip foliage from the trees, leaving the squirrels exposed. If the mast harvest is good, they grow more rapidly than did the winter-born nestlings; and since their elders are not immediately swept up into another round of mating, they may stay with their mothers in family dens throughout the late fall.

Aggregations of adults and young can be found holed up together until winter breeding is well under way, as many as nine squirrels providing central heating in one den. But first the abundant food must be gathered and either eaten to build protective bodily fat stores or buried for later use. Young squirrels attempt to bury food as soon as they start to feed on the ground. They must compete for the wood-

Acorns from the white oak seem to taste best. Bitterness is caused by tannin, and acorns from different oak species (and even from individual trees) vary in the proportions of tannin, sugars, and water they contain. This may explain why squirrels will feed most heavily on one particular tree.

land bounty with many other forest dwellers, including their sciurid relatives—the red squirrel, fox squirrel, chipmunk, and flying squirrel. The white-tailed deer and the black bear consume more acorns in one night than a gray squirrel can eat in a month. The wild turkey dines on many of the gray squirrel's favorite foods, and the raccoon is ever alert to the prospect of a squirrel-food meal or a meal of squirrel.

Crumpled-ear brought her July-born family down to the fallen acorns as September ended. At first they found difficulty in handling and peeling the larger ones, and they fed on remains that others had half eaten and dropped. Next to their white-oak nest tree, a red oak had dropped some of its rounder acorns; the mother squirrel rejected these, but the youngsters began by picking at everything. Red-oak acorns are bitter to the taste, and squirrels often pass them by until other food is used up. Black-oak acorns are less bitter, but squirrels seem to prefer above all those from the white oak.

Young squirrels do not bury their food well at first. In sweeping the duff over it, the acorn is often uncovered and left exposed. Or they will take a recently buried acorn from storage and eat it or rebury it elsewhere.

When the mast crop is large, squirrels often seem to have foreseen —as early as June—that autumn would bring plenty. In such years many summer young are born, whereas a failure in crops of white-oak acorns, beechnuts, and other foods is preceded by poorer breeding among squirrels. Old-time accounts of mass migrations often mention that they preceded an autumn of food shortage. Food supply, breeding, and emigrations are apparently linked, but the pattern is not a simple one.

The gray squirrel migrations which so impressed the early settlers were not uncommon. Audubon and Bachman suggested in 1870 that it be called *Sciurus migratorius,* "it being the only one in our country that appears to possess this peculiarity." (It is a peculiarity shared by the Russian red squirrel, however, which is supposed to be its nearest relative.) The general belief at first was that the animals were searching for food and that they returned afterward to the places from which they came; Peter Kalm, a Swedish scientist and traveler, added this conclusion to his account of a southward migration of squirrels in Pennsylvania in 1749. The naturalist Ernest Thompson Seton calculated that mass movement from Iowa to Wisconsin in 1842 involved a half billion gray squirrels; he thought that such treks were caused either by infestations of fleas or by some psychological factor. Certainly a willingness to enter water was mentioned in many accounts. Robert Kennicott wrote in 1856 that, in Wisconsin and Michigan, "immense numbers congregate in autumn, and move off together, continuing their progress in the same general direction, whatever it may be, not even turning aside for large streams." This account makes another point, that migrations take place in the fall, when food is at its annual high in normal years.

Mass movements were recorded in southern states, too. Johann D. Schöepf wrote how, in 1780, squirrels poured from Kentucky toward the coast. "Failure of the nuts and acorns, it was said, was the reason for this migration . . . it was prophesied at the time that a hard winter would follow, and in reality this was the case."

Some characteristics are common to almost all migration accounts, whatever the state or the century. Movement starts in September or October, following a year of abundant mast and when the current crop of nuts is poor. Squirrels are scarce for a time afterward but in a

Pin-oak acorns and others may be used as food when the white-oak crop is killed by a late spring frost. There is a rough correlation between gray squirrel "migration years" and years when abundant acorn crops are succeeded by very poor ones; an irregular rhythm of about five years has been noticed in northern states. But not every year of abundance is followed by a movement year, and not all years of food shortage produce migrations.

few years may have built up again. A large proportion of the travelers are killed or die en route. Many descriptions remark upon the fearless and unusual behavior of the traveling squirrels, which maintain the direction of travel despite many obstacles.

There is no evidence that the travelers return, so it is best to call such phenomena emigrations rather than migrations, more akin to the movements of lemmings than to the seasonal journeys of birds. Unlike birds, squirrels and lemmings are not moving toward longer daylight and warmer temperatures; and if it is simply food that they are seeking, they should be in poor condition at the start of their journeying. This is not the case; they usually begin to move while still plump and before food shortages are acute.

During the past hundred years mass movements of gray squirrels have become more rare, but there have been recent instances: in September, 1960, an unusual number of dead squirrels was seen on the Massachusetts Turnpike; in the fall of 1964 there was an emigration in north Georgia; and in 1968 in mid-September there was abundant evidence that in many of the eastern states squirrels were once again on the move.

O. H. Monroe, the Allatoona Reservoir Manager in north Georgia, described peak movements there during October and November of

76

1964. He said that large numbers of dead squirrels were found along the south shoreline, the bodies of many squirrels were observed on highways throughout the area, and citizens of Cartersville remarked frequently on the large numbers of the animals found within the city limits. The squirrels crossed the reservoir from north to south; when one encountered a boat while swimming, it ran up a paddle and across the shoulders of the man in the boat, re-entered the water, and continued toward the south shore. Although there were fox squirrels in the neighborhood, none was observed to take part in the movement. Mr. Monroe remarked that there was little or no mast in the district, as a late spring freeze had killed the oak and hickory blooms the preceding spring.

Several million squirrels are likely to have been involved. Joseph Kight, of the Georgia Game and Fish Commission, noticed that there were very few summer young in the fall population, possibly because poor spring and summer foods prevented breeding or because young were lost after birth. In August and September, well before the mass movement became obvious, gray squirrels seemed to be unusually restless and incautious, wandering aimlessly on the ground. Kight collected several squirrels just before the emigration and noticed that they had little or no body fat and that most were in poor physical condition.

As many as twenty million squirrels were involved in the 1968 emigration, which covered an area of several hundred thousand square miles: North and South Carolina, Tennessee, Kentucky, Georgia, Alabama, Virginia, Pennsylvania, and New York, between latitudes 33 to 43 degrees north and longitudes 75 to 90 degrees west. A newspaper report said that fifty tons of dead squirrels were removed from a reservoir in New York.

Vagn F. Flyger made a special investigation of the 1968 event, estimating that the number of gray squirrels killed on highways in North Carolina exceeded the normal road kill by a factor of more than 1,000. (After many years of observation he has decided that whenever the number of dead squirrels on highways exceeds an average of more than one per ten miles, some sort of unusual activity is taking place.) Only one of the squirrels examined from roadways and from reservoirs proved to be from a summer litter; the vast majority were young from litters born the preceding spring, and many more females were found than usually is the case among road kills. Examination of bodies showed no unusual pathological conditions, nor was there an abnormal number of parasites. No unusual internal condition was observed, and no squirrel examined appeared emaciated or otherwise in poor condition. Flyger commented that the food supply was certainly adequate at the time of the unusual activity but that there would not have been enough to last throughout the winter. He found no indication that squirrels were trying to escape areas of high population density because of social strife or that they were under any form of unusual stress.

Descriptions of their behavior suggest, however, that many squirrels were upset. Isn't all this restless casting about on the ground, dancing on the highway, jumping in the air, and zigzagging back and forth to be expected of an animal whose social structure had broken down so that it is now in the company of thousands of its kind? To understand this aspect of the emigration, one would need to start with numbers of marked animals in their home area after a bumper winter breeding season and devote hours to watching their social behavior when frost or some other force caused the oak, beech, and hickory flowers to fail in April and May and no females came into breeding condition in the summer. Perhaps it would then be possible to record whether some squirrels stay and drive the others out or if all begin to display restless movement. Does emigration really begin in September or has it been gathering momentum for months beforehand? Which, if any, of the travelers find a new home? How far does one individual travel? Do any return?

Another hypothesis would explain such emigrations biochemically. If one presupposes that diet affects the physiology of the squirrel so as to trigger off breeding in fall, the high seed-oil content of abundant mast might influence the initiation of breeding condition both in males and females, and in April and May some other dietary factor (pollen, perhaps) might lead to summer breeding. A shortage of this spring diet factor might affect the squirrels' normal behavior in other ways than by a failure in reproductive readiness.

From the point of view of the species as a whole, several advantages of occasional mass movements leap to mind. Emigrations are ways of extending range. For a species that spread over great continuous forests, thousands of miles from North to South, and almost as far from East to West, some mechanism must have operated to prevent speciation raising breeding barriers. (In all that range, only six sub-species of gray squirrel are known, and they intergrade where their ranges come together.) Emigrations lead to wide-ranging redistribution of genetic factors.

Durward L. Allen has said in *Our Wildlife Legacy:*

The migrations, it seems, were a device for clearing the land of a too-numerous population and converting a million animals back into the humus of the earth. A part of the time, at least, the gray squirrel is sufficiently immune to the effects of external controls (disease, predators, etc.) so that in the course of the ages it has developed a *sociological* means of getting rid of its excess numbers.

This is the best guess of all.

Perhaps the production of the summer crop of squirrels and the autumn crop of food is encouraged by a common factor. If the squirrels are not tied up with family responsibilities through summer and early fall, they may be more likely to start foraging widely. We believe that the catkins (male flowers) of oaks, beeches, pines, and spruces are very important prebreeding foods for squirrels. They and

79

the female flowers, of course, determine the crops borne on these trees in fall. If the trees don't flower heavily because of "exhaustion," or because air temperatures the preceding July were low, or if the flowers are hit by late frosts and cold wet weather, squirrels will have a restless autumn and a trying winter. They may be saved by other foods; the black-oak group has acorns which take two years to develop, for example. But some years many failures coincide: a hungry autumn is followed by a cold, hungrier winter, and spring comes without the bumbling purr of young. The effects of a stressful winter and spring may continue into the summer breeding period, and there will be only one young for every three adults in the autumn population, as compared to very good years, when three out of four squirrels in the fall population may be less than a year old. In some years, autumn populations have more winter-born than summer-born young in the one- to two-year-old group; whereas in other years, summer-born young predominate. This makes us think that production and survival of summer young are influenced by the success of the previous winter's breeding.

Hazelnuts are a valuable food in autumn. They store well and can be dug out in February still moist and fresh. Eaten as they are harvested, they contain almost as much fat as the butternut, more carbohydrate, some protein, and more than three times as much vitamin A. Other useful ingredients are small traces of vitamins B_1 and C and a wide range of mineral traces; levels of calcium, phosphorus, sul-

Maturing hazelnuts are a favorite food.

phur, chlorine, potassium, and magnesium are higher than those found in walnuts and chestnuts, and they also contain sodium, manganese, iron, and copper. It isn't surprising that squirrels have perfected a special technique for splitting open their hard shells!

Most of the young gray squirrels born in summer are completely weaned during early October, and they descend to the forest floor at about the time frost touches the leaves. They will already be showing signs of the replacement of their baby coats, and a growth of silvery new hair thickens their tails. Graduate student Martin J. Barrier discovered that summer-born young differ from the rest of the population in the sequence of their fall molt—they follow the pattern typical of the spring, unlike their elders, which are molting at the same time. The coat of the nestling is always shed from head to tail, which involves summer young in two successive molts in the same direction.

Hunters may be puzzled by the various coat conditions they find among the squirrels they take early in the season, especially if they are not certain about the age classes and recent breeding history of the squirrels they have bagged. But apart from the inevitable differences in animals—always there to contradict any dogmatic assertion —the molt of gray squirrels in the fall follows one of three timetables.

In most of them it begins with regrowth of tail hairs in August, followed in late September by replacement of body hair, which is concluded toward the end of November. In adult males, females which have not bred in summer (or have bred very early or have lost young litters), and youngsters born before summer the molt follows this timetable.

In females which have been nursing young during summer and early fall, the molt has a later timetable; these squirrels can still be found in January and February with the molt incomplete; timing will be related to the dates when their young were fully weaned, but October to mid-December is their usual season. Their tails may not molt until September.

Squirrels develop white woolly patches behind the ears in winter.

The third timetable, that of the summer young, extends over the same period as that of their mothers, but the sequence is reversed. Thus, while the rest of the population begins by shedding their summer hairs first on the rump near the tail, with replacement spreading forward and sideways up the body (more slowly on the underside) and finishing on the chin, snout, and feet, the summer young molt on the head first and replacement follows down the spine toward the tail, with the undersides and the feet getting their winter coat last.

Sometimes a small detail won't fit into place. What is the purpose of those white woolly patches that gray squirrels have behind their ears in winter? If they are used for threatening, why is it only necessary to have them during the winter season? They develop in November and are lost in March. Young emerging from dens in April have them, but by then only their mothers retain vestiges of them, since lactating females molt late, so are they for family recognition? But after May or June no adults have ear patches until November, and meanwhile the summer young (complete with ear patches) have emerged in late September or soon after, and their mothers will be the last in the population to grow white patches. The idea that white ear flashes are important in late fall and winter is supported by the fact that the youngest squirrels molt head first in fall. The explanation is probably simple, but what is it?

82

There was an old butternut tree at the wood's edge, and the squirrel family we were watching began to harvest the nuts one morning early. It was the second week in October. All squirrels seem eager to get these treasures, and some years they are stripped while still unripe. When a squirrel eats one (two thirds of which is fat), some 40 percent is used as fuel for bodily processes; the rest is broken down and passed in the blood to be stored as depot fat beneath the skin, between the muscles, and to sheathe the body cavity and the heart, kidneys, and ovaries. If the fat content of available foods is low, fat must be made from proteins and carbohydrates in the body and from glucose in the blood.

Young squirrels are bullied, once they are old enough to mix with strange adults, and if an attractive food brings feeding squirrels close together a peck order develops. Dominant squirrels warn and sometimes chase the lower-ranking ones. Vagn Flyger described this social hierarchy as he saw it among gray squirrels in Maryland. He began by marking individuals with different patterns of dye and hair clipping so that he could recognize each one. He built a blind so that he could watch without disturbing them, and he fixed ears of corn on coat hangers attached firmly to the tree trunks. The squirrels couldn't carry the cobs away, and if more than one wanted to feed they had to get very close. Flyger soon found that he was not seeing random irritability but could predict which of any two marked squirrels would get chased off. Dominance went with age and sex: a fully grown male squirrel was most likely to get a good meal.

James C. Pack and his co-workers at Virginia Polytechnic Institute watched 750 social interactions between gray squirrels. They found the squirrels had a social organization which was very stable, a "linear right" hierarchy accepted by all.

Even the old males do not have their own way all the time, however. Once a female has a litter, and also during the last few weeks of her pregnancy, she will chase males away from food as well as from her nest. One tame female declared her pregnancy in this way; no one realized she had mated until her mild, submissive feeding behavior at the corn tray exploded into savage intolerance.

Young squirrels independent of the mother that meet with bullying from dominant squirrels in their range may move away. Or if the mother starts another litter she sometimes turns on her young and ejects them from the nest; they are then even more likely to move than if she herself chooses another nest. We followed twenty-two such animals on our research plot and found that they moved an average of 184 yards from their respective birthplaces and established new homesites. Others, whose movements we could not trace, may have gone outside the area. In some years there is a peak period of movement between communities or into fresh areas between late May and July. Another peak is the "fall shuffle," which may be noticed in late September and October. Young are recruited into existing groups of squirrels, and the surplus is rejected. Some of the outcasts will succeed in settling in other areas; some will die. Some will come in response to harvest calling and stay to found new groups where they have buried mast; others will travel on. The squirrels concerned are not all juveniles, and the "shuffle" is just that and not a mass movement.

Edward M. Jones, Extension Forest Management Specialist, told me that on November 21, 1967, he was deer hunting in a woodland near Tarboro, North Carolina. About daybreak he watched two squirrels in the process of nest building. The chosen tree was a yellow poplar in a swampy area with its top broken out approximately 30 feet from the ground. The squirrels were cramming leaves and sticks into the hollow of the tree. Upon closer observation it appeared that the female was doing the nest arranging while the male was bringing materials. The male would leave the nest tree, jump across to the top of a beech tree nearby, cut the beech twigs with the leaves attached, then go down the beech tree, cross the intervening space on the ground, and climb the yellow poplar, where he would give the leaves to the female. She would take them into the nest cavity. Jones was able to identify the sexes without difficulty, since the male attempted several mountings during the nest-building process. He watched this continued activity for nearly thirty minutes, and at no time did he see the female attempt to bring leaves into the nest herself; she would wait as the male made the trip and gave the leaves to her. It is unusual to have observed a pair in the actual process of nest building.

Overcrowding must aggravate the problems of nesting, breeding, and feeding, and it is important to realize that the quality of a habitat —as well as its quantity—determines when it becomes overcrowded. Flyger's squirrels, living in two isolated 10-acre woodlots in the suburbs of Baltimore, were able to coexist without social disaster at densities of five to six squirrels per acre, each having a home range averaging only 1.4 acres. Ranges overlapped, and as many as six squirrels might be sharing a den. But food was plentiful, and though the rate of disappearance of squirrels from the area suggested to him a mortality of 10 percent per month, he considered this neither unusually high nor likely to be due to emigration.

The most dramatic disappearance of marked squirrels from our research area in North Carolina coincided with the winter season

Gray squirrel trails from tree to tree are a common sight in snowy woods (photo by Dr. Ralph S. Palmer).

after a very poor mast crop. The population in December, 1960, was estimated at 468, but in April, 1961, it was only 66. We did not know why, but of the 153 animals marked and released during the fall 1960 census only 31 were caught in the spring census just four months later. During the next four years 38 more of the original 153 proved to have survived, with 2 of these living outside the research area.

In the snows of winter and early spring, when food is likely to be at its annual ebb, gray squirrels have been tracked on long excursions which were apparently food-seeking rather than connected with mating activity.

Young squirrels born in the summer may experience the first severe storms of their lives when they are fifteen weeks old or less. At this age they appear to be more nervous of leaving shelter than are the adults, which can be live-trapped on the ground if there has been even a short lull in the weather. One November storm in England raged for four days, the gales bringing trees crashing down across the roads while torrential rain flooded the fields. We visited our traps three times a day, and as we went our rounds the branches were falling all around us. We saw no life in the trees, but to our surprise we caught squirrels, probably because food was scarce after a poor acorn harvest, and feeding on the ground was comparatively sheltered. A sharp gradient exists in wind speed from above the trees down to the ground level in an oak wood. Even when the trees are bare, the wind blows four times faster across the treetops than it does thirteen feet from the ground. Predators were uncommonly active; one trap was twice turned over by a stray dog, and a fox was seen near another. We found a weasel in a trap, together with a dead squirrel. In yet another trap we took an enormous feral ferret, but there was no sign of the meal that must have lured him in.

Raccoons have been taken many times in North Carolina squirrel traps, where they look rather bashful as they crouch in the inadequate space. They can be a pest to the trapper, because their curiosity leads them to examine any trap in their path, and after a large raccoon has finished with it a trap needs expert repair.

A less attractive creature that plagues the gray squirrel is the warble fly (*Cuterebra emasculata*). One or more swellings begin to appear on the shoulders or behind the forelegs of the gray squirrel in August, and by September large patches of fur have matted over a flow of bloodstained fluid oozing from gaping holes in the skin. Most, if not all, squirrels in a local area will be affected in some years but not in others. Some will have only one lump; most will have two or three; a few individuals may have six or seven. The swellings are caused by the larvae of the warble fly, a parasite of gray squirrels generally east of the Mississippi River and south of central Ohio. The adult fly is about the size of a small bumblebee; in fact, it is similar in color and shape but less hairy. Warble flies parasitize a wide variety of animals, particularly rodents, each species of mammal having its own variety. The way in which the gray squirrel becomes infected is unknown. The eggs may be laid on logs, feeding platforms, and trails frequented by squirrels, or even on tree trunks that have been marked by squirrel urine. The eggs hatch into infective larvae that are thought to enter the squirrel's nostrils. It is unlikely that the eggs of the squirrel warble are placed in the entrance of the nest; of the several hundred summer litters we have handled only one nestling was affected, and this one, about three weeks old, was one of two given to Mrs. Frank R. Wynne to raise when their mother was killed by a car. Shortly after receiving the nestling, Mrs. Wynne noticed a small swelling developing under its chest. In about a week the lump moved from just beneath the forearm area to over its left shoulder blade. A day or two later a small opening appeared, through which breathing tubes were extended; when removed, it proved to be the larva of the squirrel warble. None was found on the litter mate, nor have any warbles been found on caged squirrels, though wild squirrels are regularly infected.

Of forty warbles that Ray Allison, of Auburn University, removed from North Carolina gray squirrels in September and October, eight pupated but only two of these produced mature flies. Larval development in squirrels takes about one month. One pupa hatched in ten and one half months, while the other took one month longer. When the warble larva emerges from the squirrel it is about ¾ inch long, dark brown or black, covered with short blunt spines, and with the breathing tubes (spiracles) on one end and the rasping mouth on the other. The dark brown pupa may reach a length of 1 inch.

We have found no record of a squirrel being killed by warble-fly larvae, but they obviously cause great discomfort and may distract or debilitate a squirrel so that it falls easily to a predator. Hunters generally throw away perfectly edible squirrels because they are infested with "wolves," as they are commonly called. (Ray Allison estimated that more than 380,000 squirrels were thus discarded during the 1949–50 hunting season in North Carolina.) Warble infestations become apparent in a squirrel population by August 1, reach a peak the last of September, and decline rapidly in October. As the cool days and frosty nights of late fall arrive, the last of the larvae emerge and the pus-filled cavities heal. Freed of this insect tormentor, the bare areas of the squirrel's skin quickly become covered with the soft glossy coat that will protect it against the cold of the coming winter.

Winter

IN LATE DECEMBER, by the time winter begins, many weeks of preparation have equipped both plants and animals to withstand it. In the woods the buds and seeds sleep in protective cases; the migrants have flown south; hibernating animals are curled in their dens, unaware of falling snow; the active animals have prepared refuges to shelter them between their necessary journeys in pursuit of food. The wind is harsh in branches stripped of leaves. During summer the buzz of insects was part of the wood's life but now their hum is stilled, and many species pass the winter in the form of eggs or pupae, dormant and protected by resistant coverings.

Going into winter in good condition is vital for gray squirrels. When bitter weather keeps them in their nests, some of their stored fat is used to maintain the normal metabolic rate, and after a day or so they must feed or risk becoming dangerously thin and weak (photo by Dr. Alberto D. Vizoso).

Gray squirrels are not hibernators. Unlike their cousins the wood-chucks, no tree squirrels can put themselves into cold storage and sleep through weeks or months with their life processes slowed down to burn the minimum of fuel. A layer of stored fat, and the stamina it gives, is for the squirrel a lifeline across the stormy days of winter and early spring. The good days maintain it, but enforced fasting uses it up. Then the squirrel may become too weak to leave the den or, if it does go, it may fall to a predator or die as a result of exposure. Persistent snowfall between December and March has often warned the hunter that next fall's squirrel crop may be poor.

Now the squirrel benefits from the triple overcoat it wears. Under the skin, there is a layer of fat. Next, a soft dense underfur of crinkled hairs traps the air, acting like an eiderdown to prevent icing on the skin. Outside this layer there is a covering of coarser, smoother hairs which guard the underfur and keep it from matting or soiling, which might rob it of its insulating properties. Apart from the head and neck, the squirrel's body in winter is covered by hairs which are everywhere ⅛ inch longer than those of the summer coat, and the long hairs of the tail average ¼ inch longer.

The winter pelage is not really gray at all, although it is grayer than the summer coat and has a deeper pile. A yellow-brown stripe 1 inch or more wide runs down the squirrel's spine from its head and shoulders to its rump. The upper surfaces of its feet have golden patches, and a reddish streak marks each of its sides from armpit to hip. If the squirrel were being watched from overhead, it would still look brownish, but its outline would be softened by whitish-gray. This is the color of its legs, shoulders, and hips and of its sides between the spinal stripe and the armpit streak. Its underparts seem snowy white.

The squirrel's tail is a winter wonder. When it spreads, the long glossy hairs fluff out in different planes so that their white ¼-inch tips make the whole tail look frosted with silver. When it is flat rather than fluffed, the tail is a black and yellow striped ribbon edged with white, measuring about 4 inches across. On the lower surface, the mid-rib is kept warm by shorter hairs and underfur. As the year wears on, the tail hairs become dull, rubbed, or lost, and the result is less impressive.

The hairs of the squirrel's coat show an immense variety of length and color banding. Some of the long guard hairs on the tail have as many as nine color bands. Even the short "white" hairs of the belly have a charcoal band at the base; and the "white" patches behind the ears consist of hairs that are banded black-white-black, although the black bands are very short. Martin J. Barrier distinguished twenty-seven different color types of hair on the normally colored gray squirrel. Most of them were banded, and the colors of the bands were black, brown, or white, in different combinations. He found some purely black hairs, and on the squirrels' wrists and ankles he found short vibrissae that were a pure white. He failed to find any purely brown hair.

When a squirrel has an aggressive encounter with another, it may "raise its hackles" in a broad line down its back. Most noticeable then are the long black or black-tipped guard hairs. From one to seven color zones can be found on the guard hairs of the body, and the underfur may have hairs of one color or hairs with two, four, or five different bands. Vibrissae may be solid black, like those on the muzzle, or they may have two, three, or four bands of color or be solid white. The tail has long guard hairs with color bands numbering two, four, six, seven, eight, or nine; and underfur on the tail may have two or four bands.

But not a *gray* hair can be found!

The hair on the squirrel's body varies in length from place to place. Longest of all are the whiskers (2¾ inches) and next come the hairs of the tail. The hair on the hips is longer than that on the shoulder, with the shortest hairs being those on the head and feet. The under-

A female views her surroundings from the den in which her winter litter will be born.

side of the squirrel is clothed with noticeably longer hairs in winter than in summer.

Even before the winter solstice comes, squirrels are anticipating the spring. Many males are in full breeding condition again, but any mating now will launch the young into an unfriendly world, even allowing fourteen weeks between conception and weaning.

On the very first day of the new year a buck squirrel sniffed closely at a branch and then went slowly down a trunk, raptly attentive to some invisible trail. The wind was rattling frost-hardened leaves above its head, but it did not look up. As it dropped to the ground, it startled another male, intent on some feature of the root buttresses; they leaped apart with a loud *squee—char,* teeth chattering and claws tearing bark as one sprang up the tree again.

Two trees away, Crumpled-ear was in her den in the white oak. She had a family of four: three of the young surviving from her summer brood, and a solitary remaining female from the spring. She had returned from feeding less than an hour before, having chipped away at bark on a well-scarred maple, and found the fat pupa of a moth under loose bark near her den. She had scratched out a hazelnut and eaten that very quickly, while perched on a stump. Then she had found a vein of soft rot in the stump, which she excavated and ate, together with the insect life it held. Between each feeding period she groomed, licking and nibbling and shaking herself. In this way, and when she urinated, she left the evidence of her approaching oestrus.

Gray squirrels in the northern districts of their wide North American range might be expected to breed at a much later date in the winter than their southern counterparts. Surprisingly, the dates in North Carolina are not very different from any that have been quoted elsewhere. There is some variation between regions, and between years, but the peaks of breeding occur within a month of each other in winter and again in summer, and in all localities the ending of breeding in the fall appears to take place at about the same time.

The siring of gray squirrel litters is spread over the whole season of winter, but two State University students, Robert F. Soots and N. Britt Smith, found that 75 percent of winter litters in North Carolina were sired between December 18 and January 14. The concentration of mating is more likely to be due to a large proportion of females coinciding in their oestrus season than to the condition of the males, many of which are fertile in any month. The duration of the oestrus condition in a female gray squirrel, if it does not mate, is unknown for those in the wild—simply because mating promptly takes place. It may well be less than a day. Males become interested in the females that are in the preceding (pre-oestrus) phase, and it may even be that (as in some other rodents) the "testing" and chasing activities of the males bring about full oestrus.

Soon after copulation a waxy plug forms to close the vaginal opening. This is a sure sign that mating has occurred recently, for it persists only a short while, perhaps thirty-six hours. The plug probably consists of secretion from the male's Cowper's gland, which seals the semen in.

After mating there is a period of thirteen to seventeen weeks (while pregnancy, lactation, and molting take place) before females normally experience oestrus again. This is obviously desirable for the species, for it allows time for the mother to safeguard its first litter, but there are cases in which an actively lactating female has been found to be pregnant. However, the normal pattern is for a female to have the first oestrus in early January, mate and then carry its young for six weeks, suckle them closely for seven weeks and partially for a further three, complete its molt sometime during the next three weeks, and then experience a second period of oestrus. If it is mated, its final litter of young will be weaned the third week in September, and it will then molt but not have a third oestrus. Of course, the inevitable exceptions have been found, with three pregnancies in a twelve-month period. But females usually have a resting period, or anoestrus, during October and November and the first half of December.

If no resting period intervened, and three families were reared in succession, the third litter would emerge in the hungriest part of winter. To fit in three breeding seasons, time spent caring for young would need to be curtailed in each season.

The gray squirrel produces fewer young per female per year than most other species of small mammals. One eccentric squirrel—a captive female owned by W. C. Koon of Monongah, West Virginia—had a litter of eight in the spring followed by one of nine in the autumn, and refuge manager Ollie J. Thompson found a wild female from the Uwharrie Mountains of North Carolina which had a litter of eight. But the more typical production per year is just under three young. Since relatively stable gray squirrel populations are maintained, predation and other mortality factors, although they occur, appear to be less of a regulating factor than in many other species. We suspect that the gray squirrel maintains a stable population by a sensitive breeding response to environmental conditions and a social pattern that corrects density between the breeding periods.

Evidence also suggests that it is the female reproductive response which causes the observed failures in winter breeding after a poor mast crop the preceding autumn. Males appear to develop normally, but females do not come into oestrus.

Charles M. Kirkpatrick and Roger A. Hoffman, of Purdue University, searched for a response in growth of the thyroid, adrenal, and pituitary tissues to such factors as temperature or decreasing or increasing daylight which might determine the adult male's general pattern of sexual potency; no simple correlation could be found. The resting phase, which reaches a peak among males from late July through September, seems to come in response to an environmental influence, as it affects winter-born young and summer-born young (of the year before) at the same time. Exotic populations of gray squirrels in South Africa produce young anytime between September and April inclusive; however, there are two definite peaks in September-October and January-February. The Australian colony is said to breed from October to February.

The young male becomes sexually active for the first time when it is between nine and eleven months of age, although it may exhibit sexual play from three months. The testes enlarge and pass down into the scrotum, which is clothed with pale, smooth skin and hair. There they enlarge further. By the time sperm are present the scrotum has lost hair and become blackish and rough. During breeding, the scrotal hair becomes tobacco colored, and pigmented patches develop on the skin. In July and August the testes regress and are withdrawn so that the scrotum is empty. However, they can be returned; this has happened during examination of trapped squirrels, much to the confusion of entries in the trapper's field notebook! During the time of sexual quiescence, which lasts until about the end of September, the dark, rough skin of the scrotal sacs is sloughed away, they become smoother and paler, and the hair grows back. The flaccid, wrinkled sacs could never be mistaken for those of prepuberty, however, so that even during dormancy post-breeding males can be distinguished from sexually immature juveniles.

Stories about the emasculation of squirrels are often heard. The warble fly is said to be one cause. In England the gray squirrel is said to emasculate the Eurasian red squirrel, and in its home country the gray is said to be emasculated by the American red squirrel. In Texas, old gray squirrels are said to castrate young gray squirrels. Such stories may be the result of ignorance of the squirrel's ability to withdraw the testes from the scrotum and into the muscular protection of the abdominal wall.

After September, redevelopment starts. By December, the majority of males other than young born the preceding summer may be sexually active, while the summer-born males become active in May or June. But of course there are variations, and in some seasons much younger squirrels breed, if habitat, food, and climate conditions have been good. Precocious breeding of the summer young was first recorded in England in 1954, and in North Carolina we witnessed a similar response in 1966. In both cases, the fall mast crop had been outstanding, the population not above normal, and the winter mild. One female tagged as a nestling had bred when only 124 days old.

The social conventions of breeding in squirrels are difficult to determine. Although many people have watched the pairing and parting of semi-tame squirrels or of squirrels in captivity, the events they see may not represent the customs of squirrels in the wild. Pair bonding would seem to be difficult to maintain when the mates separate at least for the three or four months while the female is in advanced pregnancy and caring for her young, yet one of our marked males in North Carolina was found in a nest box with the same female before and after her pregnancy, and neither one was ever found with a different partner in all our checks over almost eighteen months.

Durward L. Allen had evidence that a male fox squirrel would

A mated pair.

share a nest with its mate during breeding and might be found nearby during the time that the female was denned up with young. Such behavior could lead to successive matings of the same pair. But the gray squirrel does not typically behave in the same way; adult males are found to travel widely at the time of mating, and while females are caring for young it is usual to find groups of males, sometimes together with nonbreeding juveniles, in "club" dens or nests. A female with young will chase away other squirrels which approach her den. If males do not contribute anything to the young rearing, monogamy would seem to be of no advantage to the species, and genetically it is a disadvantage. The same male may attempt to mate with other females a short time after his first observed success, and the most dominant probably sire many litters in one season.

Jan C. Taylor made an exhaustive study of gray squirrels in an 11-acre woodlot in England between 1964 and 1969. He was particularly interested in the social structure and behavior of the population, and his conclusions about the type of community built by gray squirrels are at once surprising and convincing. The social units formed were like those of the black-tailed prairie dog. Members of a unit were replaced, usually from young born into the unit. Groups were thought to be formed either from a nucleus of a female and her young or from a number of siblings or both.

The surprising thing, at first, was Taylor's discovery that during the

97

breeding season the dominant males of the groups were not concerned in mating with the group females. Instead they became wide-ranging and were seen far away from the group's normal home ground. Nor were the other males of the group seen to mate with the familiar females; this was done by outsiders. In the best-known unit, no adult male joined the community after mating was over.

No better system could be devised for preventing inbreeding while maintaining good conditions for young-rearing and all the advantages of a well-known range. But a further perfection emerged when the self-regulating fitness of each group to its range was understood. Individual recognition ruled the group organization. Members were familiar with the nest sites and food sources in their area and with the structure of the group. Lower-ranking members were tolerated when the group's needs were satisfied within the area, but at other times they were harassed into moving or succumbed. Much of the scent-marking, tail-signaling, and other communications of a squirrel serve to announce its continued presence to other members and to maintain group consciousness.

Taylor was impressed by the avoidance of physical contact between squirrels: this is only tolerated in certain circumstances, such as nest-sharing, suckling, and occasional grooming near the nest and briefly during play, fighting, chasing, and copulation. Otherwise, when two squirrels come within a bound of each other, "fight or flight" signals drive them apart again. He pointed out that unless individual recognition among members of a group can be continuously maintained by a system of behavioral signals, the life of a squirrel would be an intolerable succession of antagonistic encounters.

Sometimes the squirrels call to each other, instead of scolding or warning. Young piping in the nest usually succeed in bringing their mother to them. A female at the verge of oestrus sounds off in the icy woods with her ventriloquial wail as she sits on a branch, back against the trunk, her paws tucked into her chest. This call of the breeding season may be given by males, but it seems doubtful. The reason is twofold: first, unless the animal's mouth can be seen, the echoing call is difficult to trace; second, when a male squirrel gives it, he may be on a feeder or gathering hickory nuts. That is a different matter, for there is another call which squirrels give when they have fed or are about to feed at a source of abundant and attractive food— to anthropomorphize, a summons to others to rally around and get the harvest gathered in. The calls are so similar that they can't be written differently, and in the woods they are heard during the two main breeding seasons (late December to February and late May to July) and again when squirrels congregate to feed in September and October. The call can be written as *quac, quac, quac, quaaaaaaaa . . . quaaaaaaaaee . . . eeeeooooo.*

Once this call is familiar, as it will be to most people who walk the woods, it can readily be distinguished from the various alarms. The intense, immediate alarm is sounded *kut, kut, kut,* in loud staccato bursts. When a squirrel has raced for safety giving this warning, it often pauses and adds *quaa, quaa, quaaee?* as well. Those squirrels listening pass on a general alarm,* a ripple of disquiet which is like the human *tut tut* but is more exactly *kut, kut, kut . . . kut quaa . . . quaa . . . quaaa.* Such general warnings continue until the cause of the disturbance vanishes. Even then, a diminishing comment is sometimes made, a slower, quieter chorus of *kuts* and *quaas* while tails flick and teeth knock together.

Squirrels will eat mouthfuls of snow in winter and will lap from water held in pockets of trees. They may not be seen drinking regularly, but their soft tissues are 80 percent water, and they must balance what they lose through excretion and evaporation. Probably half of the daily intake of water is "hidden water" in food. Hans Uhlig noticed no ill effects in two gray squirrels kept without water in

---

* Deer, birds, and probably other woods animals heed the alarm calls of the gray squirrel.—*The Editor.*

captivity for one to two months. White-oak acorns are said to provide "eight drops of water" each, and berries and fruits contain much liquid—although this may be immediately used in digesting the sugars they also contain. Succulent shoots and leaves give moisture, and under natural conditions squirrels are seen licking rain or dew from leaves. We have found more squirrels drinking in late May or June than at other times. This, in England, is when young foliage on the trees hardens off and becomes less palatable. Squirrels lap at puddles and in hot, dry weather visit the margins of ponds and streams, where their tracks may be found. When drinking, the squirrel crouches and sinks its neck between its shoulders, stretching its head out over the water and holding its tail straight behind it, an inch from the ground. Nothing appears to move except its lower jaw and throat. Afterward, it often will wipe each side of its chin on the ground or on a branch and then sit up and rub vigorously with loosely clenched forefeet at both sides simultaneously. If the feet get wet or soiled, the squirrel may hold its forepaws out with the fingers spread and shake them or lick them before grooming.

During drought conditions a group of squirrels may make regular journeys to drink at a particular spot, until a visible trail is made to the source of water. H. V. Terrill, a graduate student at the University of Missouri, found about two hundred fox and gray squirrels in two acres of woods by a pond during a drought.

Rivers and streams have figured in the early descriptions of gray squirrel habitat in many parts of their United States range. Dense deciduous growth in wetter low-lying areas distinguishes the ancestral acres of this species as compared to the coniferous forest of the red squirrel and the more open oak woods preferred by the fox squirrel. During its spread in Britain, the gray squirrel's progress was carefully mapped between 1920 and 1962; it was clearly using river systems to a large extent. Broad areas of water halted it, sometimes for many years.

Yet the gray squirrel is a good swimmer. A litter of three young that were hand-reared after the death of their mother met an expanse of water for the first time at twelve weeks of age when playing in the garden. A small lily pond with a level surround was apparently not recognized as a hazard, because two of them tried to run across it. Both made the crossing successfully, and one managed to climb out unaided. Judging by their piercing squeals, the experience surprised and frightened them.

Flyger described how he watched fourteen squirrels swimming across the reservoirs that form the southern boundaries of the Great Smoky National Park in North Carolina, distances of between 75 and 300 yards. People trying to rescue the squirrels from the reservoirs noticed that the swimmers could not be persuaded to turn back and that a high proportion were swimming in a northerly direction. This was not considered to be in response to some mysterious call of the North, however, but to the fact that most of the squirrels lived on the southern shores of these east-west-running reservoirs. The explanation of the swimmers' determination may have been that they had fixed their sights on some feature of the far bank and were heading toward it.

Stretches of water more than a mile wide are not very often attempted. (How squirrels know what distance they will have to swim is hard to imagine. Some records report that they will climb trees "to view the hazard ahead," although, of course, squirrels *do* climb trees, anyway.) In 1848, during one of the many mass movements of gray squirrels in the nineteenth century, "two acres" of them were described as crossing Seneca Lake in New York at a place where it was five miles wide.

The squirrel swims with a strong and regular dog-paddle motion, holding its head high with the mouth and nostrils clear and the ears laid flat. Its tail is just above or just below the surface, and from photographs taken through a glass wall it appears that some air may

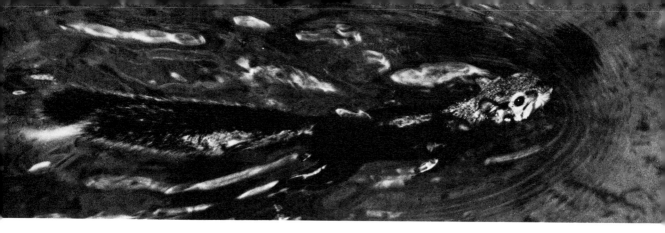

The gray squirrel is a powerful swimmer. More than one research project involving island communities of squirrels has been sabotaged by an unexpected amount of mainland visiting—by swimmers.

remain trapped in the tail, which is not thin and flat (as it looks when the squirrel leaps out and shakes) but still bushy. Certainly the hindquarters do not sink.

When it is running away from danger across open ground, the gray squirrel moves at a surprising speed. James N. Layne and Allen H. Benton, of Cornell University, timed the speed of small mammals belonging to fifteen different species by releasing each at the center of a chalked circle and recording the time taken to cross the line. (Some species needed a special course, as they would not run a straight line.) The gray squirrel was the fastest of all, beating the red squirrel, opossum, and chipmunk. One ran at 25 feet per second (roughly 17 miles per hour), and the average for six was 19 feet per second.

Jumps are often so dramatic that they inspire people to write to their local paper about the prowess of the squirrel. Estimates of the distances may not be very accurate, but after all it is not the inches that count! Nor do many people need to be told that the squirrel is a

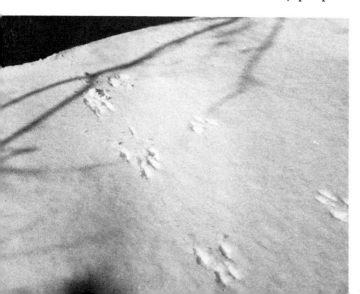

Tracks left by a leaping gray squirrel (with the lower trail leading to the tree and the upper set away from it) show the hind feet well ahead of the closely paired front feet.

good climber. One gray squirrel climbed up the side of a tall, old house with a pebbled exterior, a full 40 feet, and went in under the gable point to make a nest in the roof space. It would climb up with its legs spread a little to each side, at a walking pace. This squirrel had free run of the attic for some time before it was discovered that a Japanese tea service, never unpacked after the wedding, had been partly built into the nest. The squirrel had used the tissues in which the fragile cups and saucers were packed and had not bothered to unwrap them all.

Large expanses of window glass defeat the climbing squirrel, but almost everything else in the suburban neighborhood it takes in its stride. Cables and clotheslines are traversed, with a balancing wiggle of the tail. Walls and fences provide useful raised trailways where a squirrel may run safe from dogs and cats; in the rare event that they are not easily scaled, the squirrel quickly finds some point of access.

In Oxford, England, we had a young squirrel we prized greatly, as it had been born in captivity to a pure black mother and a normal gray father and was an interesting black-and-tan mixture. Once, it took off from the open window and ran across the roof and so onto the next roof—until it was out of sight. Every effort failed to locate it, and by nightfall we gave up hope of seeing it again. The next morning, a lady telephoned the Zoology Department of the University demanding that someone come and collect "a queer kind of monkey" that her small boy had found. She lived on the other side of town; there, safe and sound, was the ginger-and-black squirrel, looking very foolish in a parrot cage. It must have traveled over rooftops and through the city streets until it was too tired to avoid capture by the intrepid boy.

The squirrel's hands are delicate in shape but strong enough to dig and to burrow. Quite apart from the scoops made when food is buried, squirrels sometimes find reasons for making burrows. Arnold

The entrance to a snow tunnel made by foraging gray squirrels.

Bakken, at the University of Wisconsin, watched them doing this after a heavy snowfall. One squirrel began to burrow under the snow until it had made a tunnel in which it could feed. Several different squirrels used the tunnel for a day or longer, so presumably there was fallen mast or some other food in the ground litter. We have seen instances of this burrowing habit in winter and early spring, when there is little to feed from in the trees, the surface food disappears, and ice or snow prevents access to buried food from above. The squirrels must be very hungry to overcome their normal nervousness at being caught in a situation from which there is no easy escape.

Wild squirrels confined over an earthen floor will eventually dig their way out. We have seen an adult lying on its side and using its mouth and feet to tunnel below the netting walls of its pen.

When it is burying an acorn, a squirrel will run slowly across the ground with the acorn in its mouth until it finds a place that satisfies it. The first movement may be to push the acorn several times into the ground while it is still held between the teeth, or the forefeet may be used to scrape out a depression an inch or two deep before the wedging is attempted. Once the acorn is wedged, the squirrel sits farther back on its haunches and spreads its forefeet to either side, with the fingers also spread, and rakes in very quickly first with one, then the other. This brings earth or leaves over the acorn. There is no further tamping down but only a few pats with the paws. Nuts and acorns are also placed in tree holes or between roots, but there is not much evidence of deliberate hoarding at one spot. An especially attractive burying point may be used by several different individuals, but a squirrel encountering a buried acorn may retrieve its own and take it elsewhere.

Winter

When the time comes to look for buried food, a squirrel will go over the ground in a series of slow hops, nose down, like a Geiger counter. It is unusual to see a squirrel stop and dig without coming up with something to eat. Experiments with the fox squirrel by Victor H. Cahalane, of the New York State Museum, showed that moisture in the covering layer is very important in aiding relocation of buried food; his squirrels failed to locate food buried in dry sand but found it easily beneath moist earth.

The winter of 1950–51 was a terrible one for many wild creatures in Tennessee and Kentucky, for the mast crops failed in the fall and the forests were coated with heavy snow and ice for nearly three weeks in winter. A trapper in Haywood County, Tennessee, found forty-five dead gray squirrels, and timbermen in Adair County, Kentucky, saw the remains of twenty-five. Sixteen dead gray squirrels were autopsied by R. G. Brown, of the University of Kentucky, who found all to be undernourished and all but one to be infected with coccidia.

Coccidian cysts and nematode worms are common parasites in gray squirrels. *Eimeria neosciuri* is particularly common, but coccidiosis, as such, is not. It seems that young animals are susceptible but later develop what is called immunity, although cysts still occur.

Sarcoptic mange is another hazard the gray squirrel may face if winter affects its general health. This unpleasant hairless condition is

Mange and malnutrition take their toll in winter.

more often reported in fox squirrels, but gray squirrels do carry the mite responsible. What begins as a mild infection in summer may spread, as hungry squirrels den up together for warmth in winter, and rob the animals of strength and insulation.

A species of nematode worm (*Trichostrongylus retortaeformis*) was found infecting gray squirrels from widely distant localities in England, suggesting a common occurrence. Of thirty-four animals, thirty had 1 to 12 worms, one had 22, one had 30, one had 102, and another 126. Many of the worm parasites that infect squirrels are probably picked up as eggs when squirrels are feeding on the ground. In this way cross-infection may occur between species using a common feeding place; mice, other squirrel species, deer, chipmunks, raccoons, rats, and rabbits may contaminate the food itself or the earth around it. Fallen berries and nuts may lie in such contaminated ground. Bird droppings containing hard seeds are another likely source of infection; gray squirrels have been seen eating dogwood pits from bird droppings.

Not only do squirrels accidentally ingest small amounts of earth and debris while burying or digging up their food, they will also eat earth deliberately. Pet squirrels eat earth from flowerpots; one youngster repeatedly returned to nibble at the earth in a cactus garden, in spite of the spines it got in its nose and ears. There are many theories to explain why animals do this. Topsoil may provide more vitamin B_{12} than an equivalent amount of fresh beef liver, and B_{12} is necessary when carotene in plants is the main source of an animal's vitamin A. Deficiency of A leads to poor bone formation, faulty dentine, and even loss of fertility; lactating females need twice the normal intake. But the story is complicated by a need for traces of cobalt, since intestinal flora can only make B_{12} from ingested materials when cobalt is present.

The whole subject of trace-element deficiency in wild animals and the effects of varying amounts of such substances in plants eaten by herbivores is still relatively unexplored. Populations of meadow voles seem unable to tolerate crowded conditions if the soil and therefore their food is low in salt; individuals cannot survive the early stages in the population rise, whereas with ample salt individuals breed and fight and breed again.

Weather conditions have a noticeable effect on the number of squirrels that can be seen in a wood during a standard watch. This is not surprising in an animal which relies on sight and hearing and speed and agility to survive, and which lives where most travel must be done through the branches. Snow and ice hamper movement; strong gusty winds are worse. Both wind and heavy rainfall conceal other sounds; mist and fog, or a blizzard, may interfere with vision. Extremes of temperature exhaust the body. There is some evidence that close thundery weather produces disturbed behavior in gray squirrels, but it is hard for the researcher to separate the effects of weather from all the other things that may be happening at the same time. Ellis Hicks, of Iowa State University, made some very careful observations on the western fox squirrel in Iowa and found that when the wind had a velocity of 6 mph, or more, activity was substantially reduced. Other inhibiting factors were temperatures below 30 degrees F, very hot days, precipitation of all kinds, and snow more than 2 inches deep. Hans Uhlig found that gray squirrels in West Virginia reacted in a similar way.

The best that we can do is to make generalizations. The squirrel stays at home when the weather is dreadful and lies in the shade on a scorching day. But any squirrel watcher knows that his creatures do not respond very quickly when the rain begins; by the time the field notes are put away, the book is soaked!

Sometimes squirrels react to stressful events by going into shock. (This condition occurs in many species; the symptoms being low levels of liver glycogen, varying levels of sugar in the blood, and rapid or prolonged throes of death. A puzzling high blood-sugar level occurs as a temporary stage in the progress of the condition, which is preceded and followed by low levels.) Squirrels in shock behave in a confused, uncoordinated manner: convulsive seizures alternate with periods during which a hunched sitting pose is adopted with the head down over the curled forepaws so that the forehead rests on the branch or ground. The tail may be curled over the back or left lying limp. The hair of the body is sometimes erected. Convulsions are characterized by rigid extension of the limbs, the head being stretched up and back and the mouth opened in a wide gape. Death may follow in an hour or two, or after twelve or more hours. Recoveries have been observed; if glucose is given orally or by injection, such recovery is rapid. A young squirrel in shock that we took from a trap, when kept warm and given glucose, recovered and appeared very active more than a week after its release.

A gray squirrel in shock. This condition may result from capture and confinement in a live trap, overcrowding in captivity, rough or prolonged handling, frequent chasing by other squirrels, or pursuit by predators.

Squirrel and Man

THE AMERICAN INDIAN watched the squirrel long before the European settlers came. It was *fani okchako*—"blue squirrel"—to the Choctaw, and *mishe-anéqus* or *mishánneke*—"big chipmunk"—to the Natick. The Ojibwa named it *kitchi-adjidamo*—"big squirrel"—and the Cherokee called it *sălâ' lĭ,* the meaning of which seems to have been lost in the mists of time. The Indian hunted the squirrel with bow and arrow or blowgun, worried it with fire and stone ax, and roasted it whole with its guts in, but he had little effect on the swarming numbers fattening in cool forest hideaways.

On the other side of the world, a Greek philosopher gave the animal the name *skiouros,* from *skia* (shade) and *oura* (tail). In Latin this became *Sciurus,* the squirrel's generic name today. Our "squirrel" comes from variations in early English and in French: esquireul, scorel, skuyrell, and squerel.

The squirrel of mythology had a mixed reputation. Perhaps as early as the ninth century men whispered of a giant ash tree, Ygdrasil, which encircled the whole world in its branches. An eagle sat in the crown of the tree, the representative of all Good; and in the roots there was a serpent, the embodiment of Evil; in the branches between them, the squirrel scurried, bearing tales and sowing dissension. The red squirrel of Europe was thought to be under the special protection of Thor, the god of lightning, and the early Christians

109

are said to have made a ritual of hunting the animal to defy that pagan deity. But some pagans worshiped trees and hunted the squirrel because it damaged them.

Slippers made of squirrel's fur were the original ones worn by Cinderella, for this familiar nursery tale came to us from Norman-French, in which the word for squirrel's fur is *vair*. Somewhere in the telling, this became *verre*, the word for glass, which sounds the same, but surely fur slippers are more comfortable than glass ones.

The story of the sailor squirrels that instructed man to use the wind blowing across the waters is very old. Olau Magnus wrote it down about 1540, and William Byrd heard the tale from an Indian in North Carolina in 1728:

He said whenever this little Animal has occasion to cross a run of Water, he launches a Chip or piece of Bark into the Water, on which he embarks, and, holding up his Tail to the wind, he Sails over very Safely. If This be true, it is probable men learnt at first the use of Sails from these ingenious little Animals.

From James Mooney's *Myths of the Cherokee* we learn that "The meat of the common gray squirrel (să lâ' lĭ) is forbidden to rheumatic patients, on account of the squirrel's habit of assuming a cramped position when eating." And a collection of sayings by Joseph D. Clark includes: "Hunt squirrels before sunrise"; "Plant corn when poplar leaves are as big as squirrel ears" and the baffling "Squirrels bring good luck to the traveler" but "If a squirrel crosses your path, you will have bad luck."

The gray squirrel has been given a number of names. In the Southeast, it is commonly called the cat squirrel, to distinguish it from the fox squirrel; and this little cat does indeed mew when calling others to harvest or warning them of some danger. It is also known as the black squirrel and the migratory squirrel; as Silvertail, Grayback, and Bannertail. On the Eastern Shore of Maryland, it is called the fox squirrel, while the true fox squirrel is called the gray squirrel or cat squirrel. John Lawson, an early English surveyor in Carolina, was struck by the resemblance between the European red and American gray squirrels; he commented in 1714, "The next sort of squirrel is much of the Nature of the English, only differing in colour."

In rural areas from the eastern shores of North America to the Mississippi, and about a hundred miles west of it, squirrel hunting is a traditional pastime. The gray squirrel is considered to be the number-one game animal in West Virginia, and in North Carolina 3.5 million are killed annually, more than any other game species. It is probably the most hunted species throughout its range, and in the United States as a whole it is judged to be the third most important game animal. Writing of its popularity in eastern Texas, Phil Goodrum, Research Biologist, Texas Parks and Wildlife Department, said, "More people hunt the gray and fox squirrel than any other game mammal or bird in the region," and added, "The gray squirrel . . . is superior to the fox squirrel as a sporting mammal . . . and more sought after by the gunner." Texas hunters kill some 2 million squirrels each season.

The famed Pennsylvania rifle was adapted for the hunting of gray squirrels in Kentucky, where it became known as the Kentucky squirrel rifle and was used with great art to provide many squirrel fricassees. Students at Baton Rouge, when told about unwanted gray squirrels in Britain and asked for further ways by which we could reduce their number, gave the obvious answer: "Why, ma'am, you-all need six Kentucky dragonfly hunters!"

There are, of course, some states in which the gray squirrel has a lower rating in the game charts. Hunters in Minnesota take only half a million gray and fox squirrels in good years, and in Connecticut the harvest is around fifty thousand gray squirrels annually.

Henry William Herbert wrote in 1848, "Game is an arbitrary term, implying . . . those animals, whether of fur or feather, which are the natural pursuit of certain high breeds of dogs. . . . I cannot lend my humble sanction to shooting squirrels, raccoons, or opossums out of trees, and calling that sportsmanship . . ." However, there are more squirrel hunters than wildfowlers, and more men hunt squirrels than go after upland game birds.

As a training for marksmen the sport has worldwide fame: snipers during the Civil War claimed to have perfected their skill by squirrel hunting, as did sharpshooters in both World Wars. Russian snipers attributed their fame to early practice in collecting red squirrels for the fur trade, when they had to use their pea rifles so accurately that the shot entered the squirrel's eye, leaving the pelt undamaged. The equivalent for the American hunter is "barking" the squirrel. The marksman aims for the surface of the branch or trunk against which the squirrel is pressed, and the concussion causes the animal to fall senseless but undamaged. It is claimed that this can be done at a range of 60 yards.

Europeans traveling from settlement to settlement in the New World of the eighteenth century wrote many letters and diaries, and we can now share their amazement at the fertility of the land, the enormous spread of the dense forests, and the bountiful supply of game of all kinds in those days. At first, with deer and turkey so abundant, it seems unlikely that much shot was wasted on the small meat supply offered by the squirrel; but it attracted the attention of

Corn-off-the-cob, gray squirrel style.

settlers for two reasons. Wherever corn was planted in clearings cut from the woods, or along the forest edge, squirrels had to be kept off the ripening crop, or as much as two thirds could be lost. And during "migrations" of gray squirrels, many hundreds would pour out of the forests, across the farmland and the rivers, and through the villages and away.

Naturally, the colonial governments had to do something to pacify the farmers. "An Act for Destroying Squirrells" was passed at the beginning of the eighteenth century by North Carolina's Proprietary Assembly. Other acts requiring the killing of squirrels were passed, then repealed, only to be reenacted again as mast crops failed and crop damage increased. In the 1740s, Pennsylvania offered bounty payments to encourage regular hunting of the squirrel, and Ohio required every white settler to produce an annual quota of heads or tails as part of his county taxes. Communities organized contests to find the champion squirrel hunter, and neighboring townships competed in three-day events during which phenomenal numbers of squirrels were killed.

Squirrels were a significant source of food. The womenfolk showed their good sense and thrift by taking the clean meat of the squirrel and producing squirrel pie, squirrel and dumplings, fried squirrel, squirrel fricassee, and squirrel casserole.

Today this association of the squirrel with marksmanship and rural cuisine is an American tradition. But the modern Nimrod is unlikely to equal the record kills of earlier times. In one three-day contest held between two townships in Indiana in 1834, for example, one man shot 900 squirrels, another 783. Sometime before 1856, an Ohio hunter took 160 squirrels in a day, at a time when they were not unusually abundant in the locality. In West Virginia in 1862, two men took more than 180 in a day; in Kentucky, home of the squirrel rifle, Ernest Thompson Seton recorded a hunt in which twelve men took almost 10,000 squirrels in a week. These reported harvests prove one of three things, according to John Madson: "our pioneer forefathers were powerful hunters, powerful liars, or both."

The apparently boundless reservoir of game was steadily reduced as man put the land to other uses. Clearing and lumbering began in the East and spread westward through the squirrel's range to the prairie edge. Although not suffering as extreme a fate as the American bison or the passenger pigeon, the gray squirrel literally had the trees cut from under its feet. At first the ax, the whipsaw, and fire ate into millions of acres; later came sash sawmills, powered by water, and rotary steam mills. Destruction leaped forward with the introduction of the band saw in about 1880, and from then until the 1920s thousands upon thousands of square miles of good squirrel habitat were transformed into farmland, brushland, and poor second-growth forest. The saw ate the stands of nut-bearing hardwoods in the peak years of their cropping; the majestic wrecks full of cavities, the communal den trees of generations of squirrels, were cleared as so much waste.

As Hans Uhlig has said, "The old timer, whose nearest neighbor was five miles down the road with nothing but squirrels in between, is now replaced by the man who finds his squirrels ten miles down the road, with nothing but neighbors in between."

People began to feel concern about the dwindling numbers of squirrels. Before the turn of the century, as the band saw still bit into the remaining virgin forests of the East, protectionists clamored for laws to prevent overhunting. In spite of protests from farmers, who remembered what the gray squirrel could do to crops, and bird protectionists, who feared attacks on nests of game birds and songbirds, the first restrictions on squirrel hunting began in Pennsylvania in 1841 and bag limits were imposed in Ohio and Vermont in 1902. Seton reported kills in 1910 of 75 to 125 gray squirrels a day in the bottomlands of Missouri and Arkansas, but by 1919 from 15 to 20 was considered a fair bag. In West Virginia, as squirrels diminished, the 1915 season opened in mid-September and lasted to December 1; a bag limit of 12 per day was permitted, but a hunter was allowed only 100 in a season. Throughout the South there were few closed seasons or bag limits until the 1920s. Even today, North Carolina hunters can sell squirrels legally taken during the hunting season; however, the privilege of resale in the open market was removed in 1949.

The gray squirrel has adapted well to the urban parks and woodlands where his enemies are few, fruits and nuts plentiful, and sympathetic people provide food for the begging. He has been less successful in managed forests where his den trees were cut and the many food-bearing varieties and shrubs were replaced by continuous stands of timber-producing species.

A concrete spring meets a park squirrel's water requirements.

Man's Extensions of the Gray Squirrel's Range

Man has not only been the competitor and the hunter of the gray squirrel, he has also taken a hand in its global distribution. Gray squirrels were introduced to Britain from America and Canada at various times between 1876 and 1910, although they may have been tried there as early as 1830. The idea seems to have been to display them in zoological gardens and pens or, free, on certain country estates. By 1937, when their import was prohibited and it became an offense to keep them without a license, they had spread over some 21,000 square miles of England, Scotland, and Wales and were present in the Irish counties of Longford, Leitrim, Roscommon, Westmeath,

The beautiful European red squirrel disappeared throughout most of its range in Great Britain following the introduction and spread of the gray squirrel, so that it is now limited to a few coniferous forests (photo by Dr. Alberto D. Vizoso).

Damage to the bark of live trees such as this European sycamore (Acer pseudo-platanus) *by "tree rats" in Britain has led to bounty offers and other forms of control.*

and Wicklow. Today they are to be found in practically every county of England and Wales, are common in central Scotland, and have spread farther in Ireland. No mass emigrations have been recorded, although numbers fluctuate in relation to the acorn crop.

The foods available to the so-called "tree rat" are less varied than in its native range. (Britain has only two common oak species, both of the white-oak group, and no hickories.) In general, the woodlands are smaller in area and are often planted with even-aged stands of a few species. Predation and competition, as well as hunting, are significantly less than in America. All these factors have combined to exaggerate a form of behavior, already known among gray squirrels in America, which is believed to be due to sociological stress and which shows itself in the stripping of living bark from trees, especially young hardwood trees in plantations. Two species, the European beech and the European sycamore (a maple), have been damaged to such an extent in certain years that growers may have to turn to other crops, and vigorous squirrel control programs have been undertaken.

In South Africa gray squirrels were intended to fill a vacant niche in the forests of imported oaks. Cecil Rhodes is said to have liberated them at Groote Schuur in the Cape Province about 1900. In only a few years, damage in neighboring orchards caused them to be put on

117

the vermin list, and in one five-year period rewards were paid for 11,188 kills, an amazing quantity, since "only a few pairs" were liberated. Douglas Hey, Director of Nature Conservation in Cape Town, reported that the gray squirrel is numerous in the Cape Peninsula, Stellenbosch, and Somerset West districts, where several species of European and American oaks and pines have been introduced, but is still confined to the Western Cape. Recent reports say that damage to orchards is still a serious problem and that the gray squirrel preys upon several native species of birds and their eggs. Since squirrels are popular pets, Hey fears they may be transported from the Western Cape to spread farther across the country.

Australia seems to have started a colony of gray squirrels early in the century in one or more estates on the eastern borders of Melbourne in Victoria. In 1937 a single pair was liberated in the Ballarat Gardens, a short distance to the west; the curator of the gardens hand fed this pair until he left during World War II. When he returned, the squirrels had settled down and were well established. Robert Warneke, Senior Research Officer, Fisheries and Wildlife Department in Melbourne, wrote:

> I do not know how many litters they have each year but as far as diet is concerned it seems that they are restricted to areas of exotic trees, particularly oaks, in the Ballarat Gardens and in old suburban areas that have well-established private gardens containing suitable trees. They have not been able to spread into indigenous forests (mixed Eucalypt in the Ballarat area) and for this reason their present range is, literally, the Ballarat Gardens and adjacent suburbs—a mere pocket.

In Stanley Park, Vancouver, B.C., three or four pairs of gray squirrels were released shortly before 1914. By 1954 there were forty-five squirrels on 50 acres, but this population at least seems to be hemmed in by the sea on three sides and by a dense city area on the fourth.

These are the best-known instances of man's deliberate extension of the gray squirrel's world, but there are many more. On the whole, the squirrel has given a clear warning that it can survive and spread alarmingly if moved and that its behavior can bring it into conflict with man's own interests when he releases it alongside his crops.

Squirrels as Pets

If you can ignore having your furniture chewed to bits, the draperies shredded, and droppings scattered willy-nilly about the house, the gray squirrel is the pet for you. (While housebroken squirrels may exist, we have never known one.) You should select friends who enjoy being bitten when they come to visit. Your pet will climb nylon-covered legs, and its claws will test any manufacturer's claim of "snag-proof" hose. (Bare legs are more difficult to climb, but its claws are equal to the challenge.)

The adorable baby squirrel that has grown into a trying six-months-old adolescent is pitifully unable to cope with its many enemies and relations if set free. Having lost its fear of man, it will fall easy prey to a hunter. Released in town, it often becomes the victim of a cat or dog. The occasional pet squirrel that does survive is likely to become aggressive and bite people walking through its territory. Don't think wild squirrels will look after your pet; they are more likely to attack it and harass it to death.

Tuffie got his name because he was the sole survivor of a litter of four whose nest was blown from a tree during a hurricane. A month old when found, Tuffie soon became a problem. He was never vicious, but he liked to jump on a newcomer from a concealed spot above the bookcase, scurry down his back and legs, and dash up the draperies to safety before the startled visitor could recover his wits. He also liked to leap on the standing lamp and ride it to the floor.

One afternoon Tuffie was allowed to explore the yard. He scam-

119

pered about in circles, sniffed at everything in sight, and dug many small holes. After he had spent about fifteen minutes investigating the yard he decided to climb a large pine. He moved well for a short distance before he lost his footing. Tuffie didn't fall, but he looked most unsquirrel-like as he desperately hugged the tree trunk. In a few seconds he took off again, gaining confidence as he went. Reaching the crown he began to explore his new world. Soon he discovered a green pine cone. He had never seen a pine cone before, but somehow he sensed that it was good to eat. He first tried to bite it, but in reaching for it he lost his balance and nearly fell. He then nibbled all the needles away from the limb and chewed the bark around the base. When he finally cut the cone loose he forgot to hold on to it, and the cone fell to the ground.

Tuffie cut three more cones which plummeted earthward before he got the idea of holding one with his forefeet. When he succeeded he rolled the cone carefully and examined it from stem to tip. Tuffie began to chew on the cone, but not at the base as a wild squirrel would do; Tuffie started in the middle. Chips were flying in all directions as he tried to maintain his balance and cut into a cone which was far larger than his head. Several more cones were cut before Tuffie tired of trying to extract the seeds at the base of the bracts. He refused to come down from the tree that evening. It rained during the night and became quite cold. Early next morning, after his first night in the wild, Tuffie was found huddled in the crotch of a limb, a very wet and miserable little squirrel. Coaxed down by two pecans, he came scrambling from his perch—falling and tripping most of the way. For the first time, Tuffie acted almost affectionate. There was no doubt that his expedition into the wild had been something less than a success. The ground beneath the tree looked like a high windstorm had swept through it; twigs, limbs, needles, and bits and pieces of pine cones littered the grass. Tuffie had sampled every part of the tree, but none of the debris looked like the cuttings left by a wild squirrel.

Squirrel and Man

A few hours after Tuffie returned to his cage he began to sniffle; he sneezed almost constantly and his eyes were watering. He was made to swallow a sulfa pill fragment, and his cage was moved into a warm room. He was a very uncomfortable squirrel for several days, but within a week he had recovered.

As Tuffie grew older he became more of a trial. He liked to climb people and sit on their heads. His route was well marked by small bloody claw marks up our leg and along the side of our face. We gave Tuffie away that spring. His new owners released him, after having to retrieve him several times from the top of a large oak, and Tuffie was shot while raiding a neighbor's pecan tree that fall.

Fella was a blithe spirit indeed. He was always more trusting than his mother and brothers—they scampered away every time we approached the bird feeder. He was only about four months old when he first began to accept tidbits. To the call, "Here, Fella," he would

Hand-raised squirrels may be fed milk with an eyedropper.

come scurrying through the trees and down to the feeder. When full he came at a more leisurely pace to get the nuts, which he promptly buried. During his first summer he learned to come into the bedroom to get his food on the windowsill. He would eat a few pecans on the bed and then busy himself hiding the remainder in the yard. Sometimes a "tame" squirrel is actually a sick one that soon disappears from the population, but not Fella. A varied diet of pecans, hickory nuts, acorns, and sweet potatoes kept him in tiptop shape throughout the winter, but he disappeared in the spring, perhaps a victim of his trusting nature.

Pesky was six weeks old when found in a wood duck nest box one March. He graduated rapidly from the eyedropper with warm milk to a diet of cracked nuts. Unlike little boys, he seemed to enjoy having his face, paws, and fur cleaned with a warm wet rag. He undoubtedly missed the constant grooming his mother had given him. Unless the milk is removed from the fur after each meal, a hand-reared squirrel will almost certainly get a fatal case of diarrhea. (Improper grooming in the wild might also cause the young to sicken and die.) Nor is a young squirrel able to tolerate sugar, molasses, or honey, and many an orphaned nestling has been killed by being fed a formula containing them.

Pesky's growth was rapid, and by July he was as large as a wild yearling squirrel. At six months of age he became very aggressive; when he bit our secretary he was relegated to a large outdoor cage which he proceeded to defend against man and squirrel just as vigorously as he had the office in which he was reared. It was a real surprise when he accepted Donnie, Bonnie, and Connie, litter mates that were six months his junior.

Susie was only one day old when she was dropped by her mother in Mrs. Frank R. Wynne's yard. Susie was fed a formula of half cow's milk and half cream every four hours day and night, kept on an electric heating pad, and carefully washed after each feeding. Her ear passages opened in nineteen days and her eyes in thirty-two. Susie played like a kitten with a toy made of a button suspended by a string about three inches above her heating pad. She would roll on her back, claw at the button, bite it, and dash around her box for long periods. Mrs. Wynne rigged a harness for Susie which permitted her to romp in the yard, bury nuts, climb tree trunks, and exercise vigorously. Susie was shy and would dash for Mrs. Wynne whenever a stranger entered the house. She would often peer from behind Mrs. Wynne's neck, lay her ears back, and fluff her tail, all the while scolding and grinding her teeth loudly, but she never attacked. She had one litter when two years old and another when four.

If you grab a pet squirrel it is going to bite you, as will even the smallest mouse if it is so seized. It is a wise rule not to put your hands on the squirrel. Your thumbs and your ears are favorite biting spots

The "smile" isn't what it seems; this squirrel is grinding its teeth. A fluffed tail, narrowed eyes, and partly flattened ears are the threat signs of a dominant male park squirrel. An attack may follow such a display.

so keep still if the squirrel runs down your sleeve or sits on your shoulder! If a squirrel dislikes your manners, it will usually give about two seconds' warning by growling and chattering its teeth before it attacks. And if you thoughtlessly sit down just where an acorn has been hidden a few moments before, you are in for it.

Gray squirrels, like people, differ; no two are alike. The gray squirrel is playful, but only on its own terms. It reacts violently when teased. The gray squirrel's invariable response to a tightly held nut is to lunge at the hand of the holder, who is usually so startled that he drops the nut, which the squirrel quickly seizes. You may be bitten through the finger while unintentionally holding a nut too tightly. Squirrels in city parks learn early in life that the surest way of obtaining a nut is to attack the hand holding it. Scratches and puncture wounds often result from hand feeding semi-tame squirrels. Infections resulting from squirrel bites or scratches are unusual and are generally not serious, but as a precautionary measure all of the research assistants on the North Carolina squirrel project were immunized against tetanus. Rabies has been reported in the gray squirrel; the *Annual Rabies Summary—1968* of the U.S. Department of Health, Education, and Welfare says that probably "more humans are bitten by rodents and lagomorphs [rabbits] each year than by any other species of animals except dogs" but adds, "There has never been a case of human rabies reported in the United States following exposure to an infected rodent or lagomorph."

Unprovoked attacks by gray squirrels are not unusual and occur most frequently in parks and suburban areas. From Britain, the Honorable A. Hollard-Hibbert told how a gray squirrel "jumped from the ground onto a bicycle being ridden by a female servant here, then onto her shoulder. She put up her hand to take it off and it bit her really badly through the wrist. The next day a squirrel, probably the same, jumped onto one of my gardeners' shoulders— so we pursued it and shot it."

From Cape Town, South Africa, Douglas Hey wrote, "I know of three incidents of attacks on ladies taking walks along oak avenues, during 1965. Although they were badly bitten on the leg and neck there were fortunately no after effects."

A patient of Dr. John F. Weeks of Elizabeth City, North Carolina, was bitten while sleeping near an open window. The squirrel escaped before it could be captured.

Are squirrels vicious? We can only say, "This animal is dangerous: it defends itself when attacked." People may be unaware that they are behaving in a way which the squirrel may interpret as aggression. To push one away or make any sudden movement, or to attempt to hold any part of the animal, constitutes attack in the squirrel's language.

Management of the Gray Squirrel

While the number of squirrels in an area fluctuates throughout the year and from one year to the next, some woodlands will consistently have more squirrels in them than others. The ability of a woodland to support a particular number of animals per acre is called its "carrying capacity" by the wildlife biologist. One of his many jobs may be to discover why certain woods carry more squirrels than others and to take measures to increase or decrease the population as the situation demands. The manipulation of wild animal populations is wildlife management, a many-faceted activity. Wildlife management in the case of squirrels usually involves increasing the population level; however, it may mean reducing it or, in rare instances, eliminating the species from an area entirely.

To manipulate a population effectively requires an intimate knowledge of both the biology of the species and its habitat. In 1825 Richard Harlan wrote on the title page of his *Fauna Americana*, "The manor of living nature is so ample that all may be allowed to sport on it freely. The most jealous proprietor cannot entertain any apprehension that the game will be diminished, or even perceptibly thinned." But in the next hundred years the "manor of living nature" was to become less ample for many species, including the forest-dwelling squirrel.

For the gray squirrel, good living means a varied and dependable food supply throughout the year, water to drink, and hollow trees for escape and nest holes. A diversity of foods is essential for the maintenance of a high population; the fewer the species of food-producing plants, the more chance there is that a late spring frost will destroy next winter's food supply.

The moist forest floor, free of thick vegetation where enemies can hide, is a source of mushrooms, small berries, and succulent grubs and a place to store seeds and nuts. The importance of the tulip poplar, which occurs throughout most of the gray squirrel's range, is often overlooked; it furnishes nest linings, its orange and yellow-green flowers are gathered during the early spring and the nutritious pollen-bearing stamens devoured, its seeds are eaten in the summer

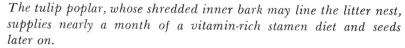

The tulip poplar, whose shredded inner bark may line the litter nest, supplies nearly a month of a vitamin-rich stamen diet and seeds later on.

and fall, and its hollows provide den sites and refuges throughout the year. The white oak gives sweet-flavored acorns, and, when they fail to crop, the black and red oaks fill the gap. Each April, catkins from these trees relieve the squirrels' winter fast. The red oak holds its leaves into December for winter nests. The hickory and butternut are thronged with feeding squirrels in the fall, and a few pines offer green and mature cones to fill the gap between summer fruits and the main mast course. In June the strawberries along the stream banks, and the early ripening dewberries and cherries, are feasted on by young and old alike. Bushes of hazel are valuable, their nuts packed with calcium. Dogwood pits and black-gum fruits and seeds add variety to the fall diet. Shrubs and plants bear foods of value, so clearings and edges along a stream or track are valuable assets. In a summer drought, when the wooden saucers of rainwater dry out in limb junctions of old trees, a pond or stream adds to the squirrels' perfect place. The wildlife manager directs his efforts toward creating these conditions, and the warning calls of squirrels reverberating through the woodland is his greatest reward.

This scene will empty of squirrels if the older trees are cut, the den-ridden wrecks removed and replaced with pine, the stream straightened and its headwaters drained. Channelized streams are unreliable water sources, the moist woodland will dry out as the water table is lowered, the squirrels' menu will develop seasonal gaps, and their numbers will diminish.

Artificial nest boxes of wood or rubber tires raise the carrying capacity of a woodland. In fact, squirrels show a marked preference for man-made dens that are dry and provide protection from most of their enemies; females have moved their young from leaf nests and natural dens into our nest boxes as soon as they were erected. Artificial structures are an expensive substitute for an adequate supply of natural dens, but in the intensively managed forests of the future, artificial nest boxes may play an important management role. Today

A gray squirrel examines a newly erected nest box.

Night checks provide good measures of nest-box use.

they are a valuable research tool because of the ease with which adult and young squirrels may be captured in them.

Censuses are a means of evaluating the effect of a management practice; a count of leaf nests is one example. If we count the nests each fall in the same woodland, we can get a rough idea of whether the squirrel population is increasing, decreasing, or remaining stable, but not an accurate estimate of the number of squirrels present.

The age composition of the population is also important, for the number of breeding females holds the key to the next season's crop. Martin J. Barrier found that squirrels in the winter coat could be separated into nestling, juvenile, subadult, and adult age classes on

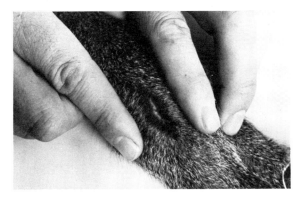

The parted rump hair of a young squirrel in winter reveals a basal portion that is dark and unbanded . . .

whereas the adult's winter pelage appears to have a light band near the middle of the parted fur.

the basis of pelage. Ward Sharp, of Pennsylvania State University, discovered that young and adult squirrels could be recognized by differences in their tails. The success of previous breeding seasons can therefore be determined from the winter pelage characters of the living animals. More accurate aging techniques are available if the squirrel is dead.

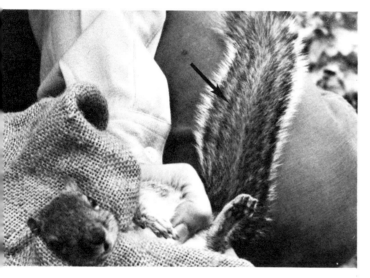

On the underside of a young squirrel's tail, the tail bone is visible, as are two or three black bars.

In the adult animal, the tail hair completely obscures the bone and there are no distinct bars.

Squirrel hunting is a popular form of outdoor recreation. The gray squirrel harvest is at least 25 million annually and can be doubled without depleting the supply if the habitat is not changed. In good habitat, hunting has little effect on the squirrel population or its abundance from year to year. This fact was driven home with forceful clarity during attempts to clear an English woodlot of squirrels. Two biologists from the Infestation Control Laboratory and a game keeper used shotguns, aluminum poles, smoke from burning rags, and two well-trained Labradors but sadly concluded, "Shooting, even when done systematically by experts, proved to be an inefficient method of killing squirrels, probably accounting for less than half the population."

Daily and seasonal bag limits have value in that the hunter who gets his limit receives a psychological boost. Seasonal limits on squirrels are unenforceable, and daily limits are of doubtful value as a management tool. A highly emotional matter among squirrel hunters (on which there is little agreement) is the best time to open and close the season. Seasons opening before October 1 result in the loss of many unweaned young when the mother is killed; however, recently weaned young may be lost to natural enemies if the opening is delayed until November 1. By January 15 most adult females are carrying young, so that a season extending beyond that date is likely to result in an unfavorable reaction from the public even though the hunting pressure on the gray squirrel throughout most of its range is so light that neither bag limits nor closed seasons are necessary to protect them or to ensure good hunting. Hunters rarely take more than 10 percent of the fall population, which is about one fourth of the number that will die before the winter young are born.

Squirrels may be controlled on a few hundred acres but the cost per animal taken is high. On several thousand acres of good squirrel habitat the cost of control is prohibitive. In March 1953 Great Britain began paying a bounty of 14 cents for the tail of each gray squirrel killed. In 1956, following a severe winter and drop in the squirrel population in 1955, the bounty was raised to 28 cents per tail in hopes that the introduced menace could be wiped out. Favorable breeding conditions occurred in the summer of 1956 and spring of 1957. By the end of 1957 the squirrel population was back to its healthy

A muslin bag may be used to remove a live trap.

1953 level, and the bounty system was abandoned the next year. The bounty system fails to control a population since few animals other than surplus ones are taken. As the population is reduced, those that remain have more food and less competition; as a result, more young are produced and more survive.

Squirrels raiding a garden can be live trapped and removed to at least five miles from the area. Since squirrels usually follow regular travel routes, traps placed in their trails are quite effective. Shooting is also effective but is generally forbidden in towns. Control is most efficient when the damage first begins, since only one or two animals are involved. A day or two after the "advance party" has located your sweet corn, every squirrel in the neighborhood will be your unwelcome guest. Squirrel damage to commercial corn or pecan groves is not a serious problem in most areas today.

Bird feeders suspended on a horizontal wire with aluminum pie pan barriers on each side will discourage squirrels temporarily, but the furry vandals soon discover that they can shake the food to the ground by pulling and swinging on the wire; a mother squirrel will teach her young the trick. The only bird feeder we know that squirrels can't raid is one mounted on a smooth metal post with a cone-shaped collar two feet in diameter mounted just beneath the feeder. The feeder must be at least five feet from the ground and away from overhanging branches, or the ingenious acrobat will be on the feeder before your favorite birds finish their first meal. Greasing the pole will furnish an interesting afternoon of squirrel watching as they try to scramble up its slick surface. One man removed the collar beneath his bird feeder, saying, "Any squirrel that can climb a greased pole deserves a reward."

Squirrels may be screened out of attics by placing heavy hardware cloth over their entrance holes. Applying several pounds of naphthalene or paradichlorobenzene crystals around the eaves will discourage their use of the attic, and this material should be applied several days before all the holes are plugged.

By far the largest number of complaints about squirrels comes from their ability to pilfer seeds from a bird feeder. Our answer to this problem is either quit feeding the birds, get a squirrel-proof feeder, or, best of all, join the ever-increasing army of citizen squirrel watchers.

Squirrel watching is fun.

Distribution of the subspecies of the gray squirrel, Sciurus carolinensis, *in the United States.*

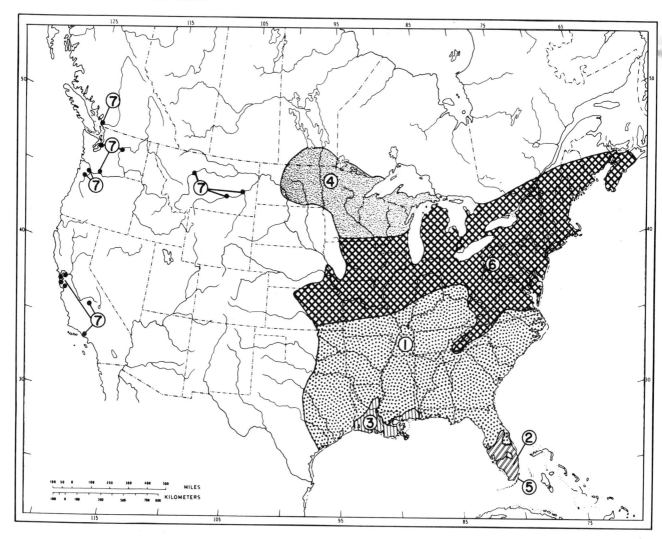

Distribution of <u>Sciurus carolinensis</u>

1. <u>S</u>. <u>c</u>. **carolinensis**
2. <u>S</u>. <u>c</u>. **extimus**
3. <u>S</u>. <u>c</u>. **fuliginosus**
4. <u>S</u>. <u>c</u>. **hypophaeus**
5. <u>S</u> <u>c</u>. **matecumbei**
6. <u>S</u> <u>c</u>. **pennsylvanicus**
7. <u>S</u>. <u>c</u>. **(Introduced)**

Subspecies of the Gray Squirrel

Gray squirrels occupy the eastern half of the United States, including many islands off the Atlantic and Gulf coasts. Their range in Canada, which originally included only the southernmost part of Ontario, has been extended northward by introductions into southern Quebec, New Brunswick, British Columbia, and Nova Scotia. Isolated colonies of introduced gray squirrels have also become established in California, Oregon, Washington, and Montana in the United States and in Ballarat and Melbourne in southern Australia. The species is well established and considered a pest in South Africa, England, Wales, Scotland, and Ireland.

Distribution of the gray squirrel, Sciurus carolinensis, *in Great Britain and Ireland.*

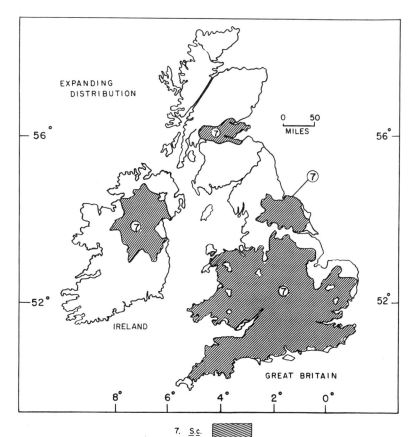

7. <u>S.c.</u>

Six subspecies of gray squirrels are recognized. Subspecific differences are not clear-cut, so that even adult specimens from the type locality of a subspecies (the area from which the subspecies was originally described) may be difficult to identify without a careful study of their pelage and skull. In general, the size and weight of the species increases from south to north. The fur also becomes more dense, finer, and longer to the north. In the southern forms, the gray-phase pelage is darker, but the melanic and chocolate-brown pelages so common in the North are almost unknown south of North Carolina and Tennessee. Not only does the appearance and color of the individual gray squirrel's pelage vary with age, season, and health but its weight may vary 150 grams or more from one season to the next according to its food supply, and its daily weight will fluctuate up to 90 grams (depending upon the contents of its stomach). Even though a gray squirrel approaches adult size and weight between eight to ten months of age, it will not become fully mature until it is approximately twenty months old.

The measurements given for each subspecies are for adult animals from or near the type locality. Measurements are in millimeters and weights in grams. The first number in the series is the average, with the number of specimens represented in brackets, and the minimum and maximum is shown in parentheses.

Sciurus carolinensis carolinensis Gmelin—Carolina gray squirrel. Range: Central Florida to southern Virginia, westward to south-central Kansas, eastern Oklahoma, and Texas.

Measurements: Total length—460 [28] (440–490); tail vertebrae —207 [28] (192–238); hind foot—65 [36] (60–67); ear—31 [36] (28–33); weight—474 [34] (300–590).

S. c. carolinensis is the most numerous and has the most extensive range of the six subspecies. It intergrades in a wide band along its northern boundary with *S. c. pennsylvanicus,* and with *S. c. fuliginosus* and *S. c. extimus* in the South.

Subspecies of the Gray Squirrel

Sciurus carolinensis extimus Bangs—Everglade gray squirrel. Range: Brevard County, Florida, southward to the tip of the Florida mainland.

Measurements: Total length—430 [30] (380–475); tail vertebrae—193 [31] (159–215); hind foot—58 [30] (54–69); ear—29 [18] (25–32); weight—366 [11] (320–449).

S. c. extimus is the smallest and darkest of the mainland forms which intergrades with *S. c. carolinensis* across central Florida from Brevard County northward.

Sciurus carolinensis matecumbei H. H. Bailey—Key gray squirrel. Range: Known only from Key Largo and Plantation Key, Monroe County, Florida.

Measurements: Total length—416 [30] (383–438); tail vertebrae—190 [30] (150–207); hind foot—56 [31] (53–60); ear—30 [26] (24–32); weight—361 [13] (338–384).

The smallest, least numerous, and darkest of the six subspecies, the Key gray squirrel is an insular form that is reproductively isolated from its nearest relative, the Everglade gray squirrel. Habitat destruction and the possibility of the introduction of the larger mainland forms pose a threat to the survival of this subspecies. John P. Hubbard and Richard C. Banks believe that the squirrels on Key Largo and Plantation Key are not sufficiently distinct to warrant recognition as a separate subspecies *S. c. matecumbei* but should be classified as *S. c. extimus* instead. Until a thorough study is made of all the subspecies of *S. carolinensis,* we feel that the name *S. c. matecumbei* should be retained for this insular form.

Sciurus carolinensis fuliginosus Bachman—Bayou gray squirrel. Range: Gulf Coast of Louisiana, Mississippi, and Alabama to Mobile Bay.

Measurements: Total length—453 [45] (420–487); tail vertebrae—213 [45] (190–250); hind foot—64 [43] (56–71); ear—about 31 [1]; weight—460 [462].

The colors of the Bayou gray squirrel are rich and dark, the underparts rarely pure white and often reddish-brown. Known as *Le petit noir* by the French inhabitants of the Mississippi Delta, it is slightly larger than representatives of *S. c. carolinensis* from southern Georgia but about the same size as those from North Carolina. Ear tufts are almost never present, and ear patches in winter are often buffy rather than white. Several pairs of squirrels from Mobile were released in Auburn, Alabama, about 1920 when the resident population of *carolinensis* was low; a few specimens collected in Auburn in 1939 still retained some pelage characteristics of *fuliginosus*.

Sciurus carolinensis hypophaeus Merriam—Merriam's gray squirrel. Range: Southern Manitoba and southwestern Ontario in Canada from central North Dakota to southern Minnesota, Wisconsin, and the Upper Peninsula of Michigan.

Measurements: Total length—476 [174] (312–525); tail vertebrae —220 [174] (180–243).

Merriam's gray squirrel is the largest of the six subspecies and the only one whose range extends above 50 degrees north latitude in North America. The largest members of this subspecies occur in Wisconsin. *S. c. hypophaeus* differs from its nearest ally, *S. c. pennsylvanicus*, in having broader ears with large and very conspicuous white woolly ear patches and in having the color from the back and sides encroach everywhere along the belly, leaving the white of the underparts very restricted and often mixed with gray. The belly may be white, gray, or brownish-yellow; the tail and upper parts are usually darker, and the overall winter color is more a steel gray with less of the yellowish tinge seen in *pennsylvanicus*. In winter *hypophaeus* has a dense growth of fur on the soles of its feet between the pads, a characteristic shared by *pennsylvanicus* only in the more northern parts of its range. The body fur is long and soft in winter; short but well developed ear tufts are present.

Sciurus carolinensis pennsylvanicus Ord—Northeastern gray squirrel. Range: Northeastern United States and southern Ontario. From northern Maine to southeastern Virginia and along the Appalachian chain in western North Carolina and eastern Tennessee to north Georgia, westward to southeastern Kansas, and north to southern Minnesota. Introduced into southern Quebec, New Brunswick, British Columbia, and Nova Scotia.

Measurements: Total length—484 [7] (440–520); tail vertebrae—222 [7] (190–240); hind foot—69 [6] (61–76); weight—579 [373] (413–750).

This subspecies is almost as large as Merriam's gray squirrel, but its underparts are white in the gray phase and the fur on the body and feet usually not as long or soft. The ears have definite tufts in winter in the northern portion of its range, and there are clear white patches behind the ears in winter.

This subspecies was released at Vancouver, British Columbia, where it is confined to the peninsula of Stanley Park. Ten melanistic squirrels from Rondeau Provincial Park, Marpeth, Ontario, were released in the National Zoological Park in Washington, D.C. in 1906, and a second shipment was received sometime later. They are now well established in the park and surrounding areas.

Sciurus carolinensis

The adaptable gray squirrel is truly *"Sciurus migratorius."* Through its own efforts it has spread into parts of southern Canada and westward along the rivers in the United States. With man's assistance it has become a naturalized citizen in areas far outside its original range. Within the United States and Canada hundreds of squirrels have been moved during the past century. Since most introductions are made by private citizens, often illegally, neither the origin of the animals nor their release sites are known, and even their presence is not suspected until they become well established.

Two or more different subspecies or intergrades may be released in the same area, so that within a few generations the genetic composition of the population may differ greatly from the original stock. All of which is to say: If you want to classify an introduced colony of gray squirrels of unknown origin, just call them *Sciurus carolinensis*.

Bibliography

Allen, Durward L. *Michigan Fox Squirrel Management*. Lansing, Mich.: Department of Conservation, Game Division Publication 100, 1943.

————. *Our Wildlife Legacy*. New York: Funk and Wagnalls Company, 1962.

Allen, John M. *Gray and Fox Squirrel Management in Indiana*. Indianapolis: Indiana Department of Conservation, Pittman-Robertson Bulletin No. 1, 1952.

Allison, Ray. *A Life History Study of Sciurus carolinensis with Notes on the Seasonal Incidence of Infestation with Warble-fly Larvae (Cuterebra sp.)*. M.S. thesis, Department of Zoology, North Carolina State University, 1949.

Asdell, S. A. *Patterns of Mammalian Reproduction*. Ithaca, N.Y.: Comstock Publishing Associates, 1964.

Audubon, John J., and John Bachman. *The Quadrupeds of North America*. New York: George R. Lockwood, 1854.

Bailey, Vernon. "Mammals of the District of Columbia." *Proceedings of the Biological Society of Washington,* vol. 36, pp. 103–38, 1923.

Bakken, Arnold. "Behavior of Gray Squirrels." *Proceedings of the Thirteenth Annual Conference of the Southeastern Association of Game and Fish Commissions,* pp. 393–407, 1959.

Barkalow, Frederick S., Jr. and R. F. Soots, Jr. "An Improved Nest Box for Ecological and Management Studies." *Journal of Wildlife Management,* vol. 29, no. 4, pp. 679–84, 1965.

———— and ————. "An Analysis of the Effect of Artificial Nest Boxes on a Gray Squirrel Population." *Transactions of the Thir-*

tieth *North American Wildlife and Natural Resources Conference,* pp. 349–60, 1965.

————, R. B. Hamilton, and R. F. Soots, Jr. "The Vital Statistics of an Unexploited Gray Squirrel Population." *Journal of Wildlife Management,* vol. 34, no. 3, pp. 489–500, 1970.

Barrett, Charles. "The Gray Squirrel in Melbourne." *The Victorian Naturalist,* vol. 51, pp. 108–10, 1934.

Barrett-Hamilton, Gerald E. H. *A History of British Mammals.* London: Gurney and Jackson, 1910.

Barrier, Martin J. *Pelage Characteristics of the Gray Squirrel,* Sciurus carolinensis carolinensis *Gmelin, in Wake County, North Carolina.* M.S. thesis, Department of Zoology, North Carolina State University, 1967.

———— and Frederick S. Barkalow, Jr. "A Rapid Technique for Aging Gray Squirrels in Winter Pelage." *Journal of Wildlife Management,* vol. 31, no. 4, pp. 715–19, 1967.

Black, Craig C. "A Review of the North American Tertiary Sciuridae." *Bulletin of the Museum of Comparative Zoology,* Harvard University, vol. 130, no. 3, pp. 109–248, 1963.

Brown, Louis G., and Lee E. Yeager. "Fox Squirrels and Gray Squirrels in Illinois." *Bulletin of the Illinois Natural History Survey,* vol. 23, art. 5, pp. 499–536, 1945.

Bryant, Monroe D. "Phylogeny of Nearctic Sciuridae." *The American Midland Naturalist,* vol. 33, no. 2, pp. 257–390, 1945.

Burt, William H. *The Mammals of Michigan.* Ann Arbor, Mich.: The University of Michigan Press, 1946.

————. *Mammals of the Great Lakes Region.* Ann Arbor, Mich.: The University of Michigan Press, 1957.

Byrd, William. *Histories of the Dividing Line Betwixt Virginia and North Carolina.* New York: Dover Publications, 1967.

Cahalane, Victor H. "Caching and Recovery of Food by the Western Fox Squirrel." *Journal of Wildlife Management,* vol. 6, no. 4, pp. 338–52, 1942.

Chandler, A. C. "Notes on *Moniliformis clarki* in North American Squirrels." *Journal of Parasitology,* vol. 33, no. 3, pp. 278–81, 1947.

Bibliography

Chitty, Dennis. "A Note on Shock Disease." *Ecology,* vol. 40, no. 4, pp. 728–31, 1959.

Citron, R. *Appalachian Squirrel Migration, Appalachian Mountain Areas.* Washington, D.C.: Smithsonian Institution, Center for Short-lived Phenomena, 1968.

Clark, Gordon M. *"Hepatozoon griseiscuri* n. sp.; a New Species of Hepatozoon from the Gray Squirrel (*Sciurus carolinensis* Gmelin, 1788), with Studies on the Life Cycle." *Journal of Parasitology,* vol. 44, no. 1, pp. 52–63, 1958.

————. "Parasites of the Gray Squirrel." *Proceedings of the Thirteenth Annual Conference of the Southeastern Association of Game and Fish Commissioners,* pp. 368–73, 1959.

Clark, Joseph D. *Beastly Folklore.* Metuchen, N.J.: The Scarecrow Press, 1968.

Colinvaux, P. A. "Bering Land Bridge: Evidence of Spruce in Late Wisconsin Times." *Science,* vol. 156, no. 3773, pp. 380–83, 1967.

Constantinides, P. C., and Niall Carey. "The Alarm Reaction." *Scientific American,* vol. 180, no. 3, pp. 20–23, 1949.

Cordes, Carroll Lloyd. *Home Range and Movements of the Eastern Gray Squirrel,* Sciurus carolinensis carolinensis *Gmelin, in Wake County, North Carolina.* M.S. thesis, Department of Zoology, North Carolina State University, 1965.

Cory, Charles B. "The Mammals of Illinois and Wisconsin." *Field Museum of Natural History, Zoological Series,* vol. 11, no. 153, pp. 1–502, 1912.

Cowan, Ian McTaggart, and Charles J. Guiguet. *The Mammals of British Columbia.* Victoria, B.C.: British Columbia Provincial Museum, Handbook No. 11, 1956.

Dasgupta, B., and K. Meedeniya. "The Vector of *Hepatozoon sciuri."* *Parasitology,* vol. 48, no. 4, pp. 419–22, 1958.

Davis, D. H. S. "Notes on the Status of the American Grey Squirrel (*Sciurus carolinensis* Gmelin) in the South-western Cape (South Africa)." *Proceedings of the zoological Society of London,* vol. 120, pp. 265–68, 1950.

DeCoursey, Patricia J. "Effect of Light on the Circadian Activity

Rhythm of the Flying Squirrel, *Glaucomys volans.*" *Zeitschrift für vergleichende Physiologie,* Bd. 44, pp. 331–54, 1961.

Diem, Konrad, ed. *Documenta Geigy.* Scientific Tables, 6th ed. Ardsley, N.Y.: Geigy Chemical Corporation, Geigy Pharmaceuticals, 1962.

Doutt, J. Kenneth, Caroline A. Heppenstall, and John E. Guilday. *Mammals of Pennsylvania.* Harrisburg, Pa.: The Pennsylvania Game Commission, 1966.

Elton, Charles S. *The Pattern of Animal Communities.* London: Methuen & Co., Ltd., 1966.

Fitzwater, William D., Jr. "Color Marking of Mammals, with Special Reference to Squirrels." *Journal of Wildlife Management,* vol. 7, no. 2, pp. 190–92, 1943.

———— and W. J. Frank. "Leaf Nests of Gray Squirrels in Connecticut." *Journal of Mammalogy,* vol. 25, no. 2, pp. 160–70, 1944.

Flyger, Vagn F. *The Social Behavior and Populations of the Gray Squirrel* (Sciurus carolinensis *Gmelin*) *in Maryland.* Ph.D. thesis, Division of Vertebrate Ecology, School of Hygiene and Public Health, The Johns Hopkins University, 1955.

————. *The 1968 Squirrel "Migration" in the Eastern United States.* College Park, Md.: University of Maryland, Natural Resources Institute, Contribution no. 379, 1968.

Freeman, R. B. "The Distribution of *Orchopeas wickhami* Baker in Relation to Its Host the American Grey Squirrel." *Entomologist's Monthly Magazine,* vol. 77, pp. 87–89, 1941.

Friedman, M. H., and W. A. Turner. "Nutrition and Reproduction." *Yearbook 1939.* Washington, D.C.: U.S. Department of Agriculture, pp. 482–91, 1939.

Gmelin, Johann Friedrich. *Caroli A. Linné Systema Naturae.* Leipzig: George Emanuel Beer, ed. 13, vol. 1, 1788.

Goodrum, Phil D. *A Population Study of the Gray Squirrel in Texas.* College Station, Tex.: Texas Agricultural Experiment Station, Bulletin 591, 1940.

————. *The Gray Squirrel in Texas.* Austin, Tex.: Texas Parks and Wildlife Department, Bulletin No. 42, 1964.

Goodwin, George G. *The Mammals of Connecticut.* Hartford, Conn.:

Bibliography

State of Connecticut, State Geological and Natural History Survey, Bulletin No. 53, 1935.

Grüneberg, Hans. *The Genetics of the Mouse.* The Hague: Martinus Nijhoff, 1952.

Gunderson, Harvey L., and J. R. Beer. *The Mammals of Minnesota.* Minneapolis, Minn.: The University of Minnesota Press, 1953.

Guthrie, Donald R., J. C. Osborne, and H. S. Mosby. "Physiological Changes Associated with Shock in Confined Gray Squirrels." *Journal of Wildlife Management,* vol. 31, no. 1, pp. 102–8, 1967.

Hailman, J. P. "Notes on the Following Response and Other Behavior of Young Gray Squirrels." *American Midland Naturalist,* vol. 63, no. 2, pp. 413–17, 1960.

Hall, E. Raymond, and Keith R. Kelson. *The Mammals of North America.* New York: The Ronald Press Co., 1959.

Hall, M. C. "A Third Case of *Multiceps serialis* in the Squirrel." *Science,* vol. 33, no. 860, pp. 975–76, 1911.

Hamilton, Richard B. *The Parameters and Dynamics of an Unexploited Population of Gray Squirrels.* M.S. thesis, Department of Zoology, North Carolina State University, 1968.

Hamilton, W. J., Jr. "Caterpillars as Food for the Gray Squirrel." *Journal of Mammalogy,* vol. 24, no. 1, p. 104, 1943.

————. *The Mammals of the Eastern United States.* Ithaca, N.Y.: Comstock Publishing Company, 1943.

Harkema, R. "The Parasites of Some North Carolina Rodents." *Ecological Monographs,* vol. 6, no. 2, pp. 151–232, 1936.

Harlan, Richard. *Fauna Americana, Being a Description of the Mammiferous Animals Inhabiting North America.* Philadelphia: Anthony Finley, 1825.

Harris, Alva H. *A Study of Gray Squirrel Populations on Experimental Nest Box Areas.* M.S. thesis, Department of Zoology, North Carolina State University, 1958.

Hatt, R. T. "The Red Squirrel: Its Life History and Habits, with Special Reference to the Adirondacks of New York and the Harvard Forest." *Roosevelt Wild Life Annals,* vol. 2, no. 1, pp. 4–146, 1929.

Hauser, Doris C. "Anting by Gray Squirrels." *Journal of Mammalogy*, vol. 45, no. 1, pp. 358–59, 1964.

Herbert, Henry William. *Frank Forester's Field Sports of the United States and British Provinces, of North America.* New York: Stringer and Townsend, vol. 1, 1849.

Hibbard, Edmund A. "Range and Spread of the Gray and the Fox Squirrels in North Dakota." *Journal of Mammalogy*, vol. 37, no. 4, pp. 525–31, 1956.

Hicks, Ellis A. "Ecological Factors Affecting the Activity of the Western Fox Squirrel." *Ecological Monographs*, vol. 19, no. 4, pp. 287–302, 1949.

Hoffman, Robert S., Philip L. Wright, and F. E. Newby. "The Distribution of Some Mammals in Montana." *Journal of Mammalogy*, vol. 50, no. 3, pp. 579–604, 1969.

Hoffman, Roger A., and Charles M. Kirkpatrick. "An Analysis of Techniques for Determining Male Squirrel Reproductive Development." *Transactions of the Twenty-first North American Wildlife Conference*, pp. 346–55, 1956.

———. "Current Knowledge of Tree Squirrel Reproductive Cycles and Development." *Proceedings of the Thirteenth Annual Conference of the Southeastern Association of Game and Fish Commissioners*, pp. 363–67, 1959.

Hopkins, D. M. "Cenozoic History of the Bering Land Bridge." *Science*, vol. 129, no. 3362, pp. 1519–28, 1959.

Hubbard, John P., and Richard C. Banks. "The Types and Taxa of Harold H. Bailey." *Proceedings of the Biological Society of Washington*, vol. 83, no. 30, pp. 321–32, 1970.

Jackson, Hartley H. T. *Mammals of Wisconsin.* Madison, Wis.: University of Wisconsin Press, 1961.

Johnson, George Lindsay. "Contributions to the Comparative Anatomy of the Mammalian Eye, Chiefly Based on Ophthalmoscopic Examination." *Philosophical Transactions of the Royal Society of London*, ser. B, vol. 194, pp. 1–82, 1901.

Kahmann, Hermann. "Untersuchungen über die Linse, die Zonula Ciliaris, Refraktion und Akkommodation von Saügetieren."

Zoologische Jahrbücher, vol. 48, no. 3, pp. 509–88, 1930.

Kalm, Peter. *Travels in North America* (1770). New York: Dover Publications, 1966.

Kennicott, Robert. "Quadrupeds of Illinois Injurious and Beneficial to the Farmer." Executive Document 65, 34th Congress, 3rd Session, Report of the Committee on Patents 1856, pp. 52–110, 1857.

King, J. A. "Social Behavior, Social Organization, and Population Dynamics in a Black-tailed Prairiedog Town in the Black Hills of South Dakota." *Contributions of the Laboratory of Vertebrate Biology,* University of Michigan, no. 67, pp. 1–123, 1955.

Kirkpatrick, Charles M., and Roger A. Hoffman. "Ages and Reproductive Cycles in a Male Gray Squirrel Population." *Journal of Wildlife Management,* vol. 24, no. 2, pp. 218–21, 1960.

Kyles, Alan L. *Arthropod Fauna in Nest Boxes of the Gray Squirrel,* Sciurus carolinensis carolinensis *Gmelin.* M.S. thesis, Department of Zoology, North Carolina State University, 1970.

Lawson, John. *History of North Carolina.* Richmond, Va.: Garrett and Massie Publishers, 1937.

Layne, James N. "The Biology of the Red Squirrel, *Tamiasciurus hudsonicus loquax* (Bangs), in Central New York." *Ecological Monographs,* vol. 24, no. 3, pp. 227–67, 1954.

———— and Allen H. Benton. "Some Speeds of Small Mammals." *Journal of Mammalogy,* vol. 35, no. 1, pp. 103–4, 1954.

Lloyd, H. G. "The Distribution of Squirrels in England and Wales, 1959." *Journal of Animal Ecology* (Oxford), vol. 31, no. 1, pp. 157–66, 1962.

————. "Observations on Nut Selection by a Hand-reared Grey Squirrel (*Sciurus carolinensis*)." *Journal of Zoology* (London), vol. 156, pp. 240–44, 1968.

Long, T. A., R. L. Cowan, G. D. Strawn, R. S. Ketzel, and R. C. Miller. *Seasonal Fluctuations in Feed Consumption of the White-tailed Deer.* College Park, Pa.: Pennsylvania Agricultural Experiment Station, Progress Report 212, 1965.

Longley, William H. "Minnesota Gray and Fox Squirrels." *The American Midland Naturalist,* vol. 69, no. 1, pp. 82–98, 1963.

Ludwick, R. L., J. P. Fontenot, and H. S. Mosby. "Energy Metabolism of the Eastern Gray Squirrel." *Journal of Wildlife Management,* vol. 33, no. 3, pp. 569–75, 1969.

Lyon, Marcus Ward, Jr. "Mammals of Indiana." *The American Midland Naturalist,* vol. 17, no. 1, pp. 1–384, 1936.

Madson, John. *Gray and Fox Squirrels.* East Alton, Ill.: Olin Mathieson Chemical Corporation, Conservation Department, 1964.

Matthews, J. D. "The Influence of Weather on the Frequency of Beech Mast Years in England." *Forestry,* vol. 28, no. 2, pp. 107–16, 1955.

McClelland, Ellwood H. "Notes on the Red Squirrel in Pittsburgh." *Journal of Mammalogy,* vol. 29, no. 4, pp. 409–12, 1948.

Michael, C. R. "Receptive Fields of Directionally Selective Units in the Optic Nerve of the Ground Squirrel." *Science,* vol. 152, no. 3725, pp. 1092–95, 1966.

————. "Receptive Fields of Opponent Color Units in the Optic Nerve of the Ground Squirrel." *Science,* vol. 152, no. 3725, pp. 1095–97, 1966.

Middleton, A. D. "The Ecology of the American Grey Squirrel (*Sciurus carolinensis* Gmelin) in the British Isles." *Proceedings of the zoological Society of London,* vol. 100, part 3, no. 38, pp. 809–43, 1930.

————. *The Grey Squirrel.* London: Sidgwick and Jackson, Ltd., 1931.

Miller, Gerrit S., Jr., and Remington Kellogg. *List of North American Recent Mammals.* Washington, D.C.: Smithsonian Institution, United States National Museum Bulletin 205, 1955.

Mooney, James. "Myths of the Cherokee." *Nineteenth Annual Report of the Bureau of American Ethnology.* 1897–98. Washington. Part 1, pp. 3–548, 1900.

Moore, Joseph C. "Relationships Among Living Squirrels of the Sciurinae." *Bulletin of the American Museum of Natural History,* vol. 118, art. 4, pp. 153–206, 1959.

————. "Geographic Variation in Some Reproductive Characteristics of Diurnal Squirrels." *Bulletin of the American Museum of Natural History,* vol. 122, art. 1, pp. 1–32, 1961.

Bibliography

————. "The Spread of Existing Diurnal Squirrels Across the Bering and Panamanian Land Bridges." *American Museum of Natural History Novitates,* no. 2044, pp. 1–26, 1961.

Mosby, H. S. "The Influence of Hunting on the Population Dynamics of a Woodlot Gray Squirrel Population." *Journal of Wildlife Management,* vol. 33, no. 1, pp. 59–73, 1969.

Mullen, David A. "Reproduction in Brown Lemmings (*Lemmus trimucronatus*) and Its Relevance to Their Cycle of Abundance." *University of California Publications in Zoology,* vol. 85, pp. 1–24, 1968.

Muul, Illar. "Day Length and Food Caches." *Natural History Magazine,* vol. 74, no. 3, pp. 22–27, 1965.

———— and J. W. Alley. "Night Gliders of the Woodlands." *Natural History Magazine,* vol. 72, no. 5, pp. 18–25, 1963.

Nichols, J. T. "Food Habits and Behavior of the Gray Squirrel." *Journal of Mammalogy,* vol. 39, no. 3, pp. 376–80, 1958.

Nixon, C. M., D. M. Worley, and M. W. McClain. "Food Habits of Squirrels in Southeastern Ohio." *Journal of Wildlife Management,* vol. 32, no. 2, pp. 294–305, 1968.

Ognev, S. I. *Mammals of the U.S.S.R. and Adjacent Countries: Vol. 5, Rodents.* Jerusalem: Israel Program for Scientific Translations, 1963.

Oldham, J. N. "Studies on Parasites of the Grey Squirrel from South Eastern England: (I) Helminth Parasites." *Journal of Helminthology,* R. T. Leiper Supplement, pp. 127–30, 1961.

Orzoga, J. J., and C. J. Phillips. *Mammals of Beaver Island, Michigan.* East Lansing, Mich.: Michigan State University, Publications of the Museum, vol. 2, no. 6, pp. 305–48, 1964.

Pack, James C., H. S. Mosby, and P. B. Siegel. "Influence of Social Hierarchy on Gray Squirrel Behavior." *Journal of Wildlife Management,* vol. 31, no. 4, pp. 720–28, 1967.

Packard, Robert L. "Notes on the Defensive Behavior of Gray and Fox Squirrels While Moving Their Young." *Transactions of the Kansas Academy of Science,* vol. 57, no. 4, pp. 471–72, 1954.

————. *The Tree Squirrels of Kansas.* Lawrence, Kans.: University of

Kansas, Museum of Natural History and State Biological Survey of Kansas, Miscellaneous Publication 11, 1956.

Palmer, T. S. *Chronology and Index of American Game Protection, 1776–1911*. Washington, D.C.: U.S. Department of Agriculture, Biological Survey Bulletin No. 41, 1912.

Paradiso, John L. "Mammals of Maryland." *North American Fauna 66*. Washington, D.C.: U.S. Department of Interior, 1969.

Penner, L. R., and F. P. Pocius. "Nostril Entry as the Mode of Infection by the First Stage Larvae of a Rodent *Cuterebra*." *Journal of Parasitology,* vol. 42, no. 4, sec. 2 (supplement), p. 42, 1956.

Peterson, Randolph L. *The Mammals of Eastern Canada*. Toronto: Oxford University Press, 1966.

Petrides, George A. "Notes on Age Determination in Squirrels." *Journal of Mammalogy,* vol. 32, no. 1, pp. 111–12, 1951.

Pritchett, H. D. "Rabies in Two Gray Squirrels." *Journal of the American Veterinary Medical Association,* vol. XCII, (N.S.) vol. 45, no. 4, pp. 563–64, 1938.

Progulske, D. R. "Game Animals Utilized as Food by the Bobcat in the Southern Appalachians." *Journal of Wildlife Management,* vol. 19, no. 2, pp. 249–53, 1955.

Quay, W. B. "Variation and Significance of the Apocrine Sudoriferous Glands of the Oral Lips and Angle of Rodents." *American Zoologist,* vol. 3, no. 4, p. 554, 1963.

Rhoads, Samuel N. *The Mammals of Pennsylvania and New Jersey*. Philadelphia: privately published, 1903.

Robinson, D. J., and I. McT. Cowan. "An Introduced Population of the Gray Squirrel (*Sciurus carolinensis* Gmelin) in British Columbia." *Canadian Journal of Zoology,* vol. 32, no. 3, pp. 261–82, 1954.

Rue, Leonard Lee, III. *The World of the Red Fox*. Philadelphia: J. B. Lippincott Company, 1969.

Russell, Robert J. See in Packard, Robert L. 1956, p. 54.

Sanford, L. G. *Geographic Variation in the Gray Squirrel in Alabama*. M.S. thesis, Department of Zoology and Entomology, Auburn University, 1963.

Bibliography

Schöepf, Johann David. *Travels in the Confederation.* Philadelphia: William J. Campbell, 1911.

Schorger, A. W. "Squirrels in Early Wisconsin." *Transactions of the Wisconsin Academy of Sciences, Arts and Letters,* vol. 39, pp. 195–247, 1947.

Schultz, Vincent. "The Effects of a Severe Snow and Ice Storm on Game Populations in Tennessee." *Journal of the Tennessee Academy of Science,* vol. 29, no. 1, pp. 24–35, 1954.

Schwartz, Albert. *The Land Mammals of Southern Florida and the Upper Florida Keys.* Ph.D. thesis, Museum of Zoology, University of Michigan, 1952.

Schwartz, B. "Occurrence of Larval Tapeworms in Liver, Lungs, Spleen, Kidneys, Omentum and Heart of a Squirrel." *Journal of Parasitology,* vol. 15, no. 1, p. 67, 1928.

Seton, Ernest Thompson. *Lives of Game Animals.* Boston: Charles T. Branford Company, 1953.

Sharp, Ward M. "Aging Gray Squirrels by Use of Tail Pelage Characteristics." *Journal of Wildlife Management,* vol. 22, no. 1, pp. 29–34, 1958.

————. "A Commentary on the Behavior of Free-running Gray Squirrels." *Proceedings of the Thirteenth Annual Conference of the Southeastern Association of Game and Fish Commissioners,* pp. 382–87, 1959.

Shorten, Monica. "Some Aspects of the Biology of the Grey Squirrel (*Sciurus carolinensis*) in Great Britain." *Proceedings of the zoological Society of London,* vol. 121, part 3, pp. 427–59, 1951.

————. *Squirrels.* London: William Collins Sons & Co., 1954.

————. *Squirrels, Their Biology and Control.* London: Ministry of Agriculture, Fisheries and Food, Bulletin No. 184, 1962.

———— and F. A. Courtier. "A Population Study of the Grey Squirrel (*Sciurus carolinensis*) in May 1954." *The Annals of applied Biology,* vol. 43, no. 3, pp. 494–510, 1955.

Silvers, Willys K. "Genes and the Pigment Cells of Mammals." *Science,* vol. 134, no. 3476, pp. 368–73, 1961.

Simpson, George G. "The Principles of Classification and a Classification of Mammals." *Bulletin of the American Museum of Natural History,* vol. 85, pp. 1–350, 1945.

Smith, G. A. "Baby Squirrels Have Urge to Climb." *Science News Letter,* vol. 51, no. 21, p. 326, 1947.

Smith, Ned Britt. *Some Aspects of Reproduction in the Female Gray Squirrel,* Sciurus carolinensis carolinensis *Gmelin, in Wake County, North Carolina.* M.S. thesis, Department of Zoology, North Carolina State University, 1967.

———— and Frederick S. Barkalow, Jr. "Precocious Breeding in the Gray Squirrel." *Journal of Mammalogy,* vol. 48, no. 2, pp. 328–30, 1967.

Soots, Robert Franklin, Jr. *An Analysis of the Effects of Artificial Nest Boxes on Gray Squirrel Populations.* M.S. thesis, Department of Zoology, North Carolina State University, 1964.

Stiles, Walter. *Trace Elements in Plants and Animals.* Cambridge: The University Press, 1961.

Swanson, G., T. Surber, and T. S. Roberts. *The Mammals of Minnesota.* St. Paul, Minn.: Minnesota Department of Conservation, Technical Bulletin Number 2, 1945.

Tansley, Katharine. *Vision in Vertebrates.* London: Chapman & Hall Ltd., 1965.

Taylor, Jan C. "Home Range and Agonistic Behaviour in the Grey Squirrel." *Symposium of the zoological Society of London,* No. 18, pp. 229–35, 1966.

————. "The Use of Marking Points by Grey Squirrels." *Journal of Zoology* (London), vol. 155, pp. 246–47, 1968.

————. *Social Structure and Behavior in a Grey Squirrel Population.* Ph.D. thesis, Department of Zoology, University of London, 1969.

————, H. G. Lloyd, and J. F. Shillito. "Experiments with Warfarin for Grey Squirrel Control." *Annals of applied Biology,* vol. 61, pp. 312–21, 1968.

Taylor, K. D. "Some Aspects of Grey Squirrel Control." *Annals of applied Biology,* vol. 51, pp. 325–50, 1963.

————, Monica Shorten, H. G. Lloyd, and F. A. Courtier. "Movements of the Grey Squirrel as Revealed by Trapping." *Journal of applied Ecology,* vol. 8, no. 1, pp. 123–46, 1971.

Terres, John K. "Gray Squirrel Utilization of Elm." *Journal of Wildlife Management,* vol. 3, no. 4, pp. 358–59, 1939.

Terrill, H. V. *A Preliminary Study of the Western Fox Squirrel,* Sciurus niger rufiventer *(Geoffroy), in Missouri.* M.S. thesis, Department of Zoology, University of Missouri, 1941.

Tittensor, Andrew M. "Red Squirrel Dreys." *Proceedings of the zoological Society of London,* vol. 162, part 4, no. 21, pp. 528–33, 1970.

Trippensee, Reuben Edwin. *Wildlife Management.* New York: McGraw-Hill Book Company, 1948.

Tyrell, Bryant. See in Shorten, Monica. 1954, p. 153.

Uhlig, Hans G. "Weights of Adult Gray Squirrels." *Journal of Mammalogy,* vol. 36, no. 2, pp. 293–96, 1955.

————. *The Gray Squirrel, Its Life History, Ecology, and Population Characteristics in West Virginia.* Charleston, W. Va.: Conservation Commission of West Virginia, 1955.

————. *The Gray Squirrel in West Virginia.* Charleston, W. Va.: Conservation Commission of West Virginia, Division of Game Management Bulletin 3, 1956.

Vizoso, Alberto D. "A Red Squirrel Disease." *Symposium of the zoological Society of London,* no. 24, pp. 29–38, 1968.

————. "Tumour Viruses." *Proceedings of The Royal Society of Medicine,* vol. 63, pp. 341–44, 1970.

Vizoso, Monica. "Squirrel Populations and Their Control." *Forestry,* vol. 40 (supplement), pp. 15–21, 1967.

Walls, Gordon L. "The Occurrence of Colored Lenses in the Eyes of Snakes and Squirrels, and Their Probable Significance." *Copeia,* no. 3, pp. 125–27, 1931.

————. *The Vertebrate Eye.* New York: Hafner Publishing Company, 1963.

Webster, J. M. "Investigations into the Coccidia of the Grey Squirrel *Sciurus carolinensis* Gmelin." *Journal of Protozoology,* vol. 7, no. 2, pp. 139–46, 1960.

Wilson, R. W. *Early Miocene Rodents and Insectivores from Northeastern Colorado.* Lawrence, Kans.: University of Kansas, Paleontological Contributions, art. 7, pp. 1–92, 1960.

Winkler, William G. "Rodent Rabies." *Proceedings of the National Rabies Symposium,* National Communicable Disease Center, pp. 34–36, 1966.

Wood, A. E. "The Early Tertiary Rodents of the Family Paramyidae." *Transactions of the American Philosophical Society,* (N.S.) vol. 52, no. 1, pp. 1–261, 1962.

Wright, W. D. *The Rays Are Not Coloured.* London: Adam Hilger, Ltd., 1967.

Index

Squirrel family. *See also* Sciuridae
  distribution of, 16
  kinds, 15–18
State mammal of North Carolina, 15
Sweat and oil glands, 39
  on soles of feet, 28
Swimming, 101–102

Tamiasciurus hudsonicus, 18
Taste, 27
Taylor, Jan C., 22, 39, 50, 97–98
Teeth, 26–27, 38
  marks, in travel lanes, 38
Terres, John K., 50
Terrill, H. V., 100
Thompson, Ollie J., 94
Tortrix viridana, 67
Touch, 25
  by whiskers (vibrissae), 27
Tracks, 36
  walking, running, 36
Travel lanes, 37
Trichostrongylus retortaeformis, 106
Turkey, wild, 74, 112
Tyrell, Bryant, 32

Uhlig, Hans 44, 65, 99, 107, 114
Urine deposition, 39. *See also* Scent
  marking

Vision, 19–23
  accommodation, 20; flicker fusion,
    20
  acuity, 19, 22
  color discrimination, 22–23
  depth perception, 21–22; parallax,
    22; stereoscopic vision, 22
  distance, 21, 22
  diurnal, 19, 20–21; yellow lens,
    21–22
  field of, 21, 22; binocular vision, 21
  recognition signals, 98
  retina: cone and rod cells, 19–20,
    21–22

  sensitivity, 21
Vitamins
  A, 80, 106
  B$_1$, 80
  B$_{12}$, 106
  C, 80
  D, formation of, function, 55
Voice
  barks, 25
  buzzing sound, 69
  calls, 98–99
  cries, 25

Warble fly, 87–88
Warneke, Robert, 118
Warning, 25, 49, 98–99
Water, drinking, 99–100
Weather, effect on activity, 107
Weaver, Dr. David L., 45
Weeks, Dr. John F., 125
Whiskers (vibrissae), function, loca-
  tion, 27–28
White squirrel, 32
White Squirrel Town, 32
Wynne, Mrs. Frank R., 87, 122–123

Yellow lens, 20–21
  in geckos, snakes, 21
  in squirrels, 20
Ygdrasil, 109
Young of gray squirrel. *See also* Gray
  squirrel
  age determination of, 46–47
  carrying, by mother, 45–46
  description, newborn, 43
  feeding of, 122
  following mother, 45
  odor of, 38
  parasites, 43–44
  senses, 25
  sightless period, 25
  tooth development, 47–48
  weaning age, 48